Cyber-threats, Information Warfare, and Critical Infrastructure Protection
Defending the U.S. Homeland

ANTHONY H. CORDESMAN
with
JUSTIN G. CORDESMAN

Published in cooperation with the
Center for Strategic and International Studies,
Washington, D.C.

Westport, Connecticut
London

Library of Congress Cataloging-in-Publication Data

Cordesman, Anthony H.
    Cyber-threats, information warfare, and critical infrastructure protection : defending
the U.S. homeland / Anthony H. Cordesman with Justin G. Cordesman.
        p. cm.
    ISBN 0-275-97423-5 (alk. paper)
        1. Electronic data processing—Security measures—United States.
    2. Telecommunication—Defense measures—United States.   3. Computer networks—
Security measures—United States.   4. Information warfare—United States. I. Cordesman,
Justin G.   II. Title.
UA929.95.E43C67 2002
005.8—dc21   2001036311

British Library Cataloguing in Publication Data is available.

Library of Congress Catalog Card Number: 2001036311
ISBN: 0-275-97423-5

First published in 2002

Praeger Publishers, 88 Post Road West, Westport, CT 06881
An imprint of Greenwood Publishing Group, Inc.
www.praeger.com

Printed in the United States of America

The paper used in this book complies with the
Permanent Paper Standard issued by the National
Information Standards Organization (Z39.48–1984).

P

In order to keep this title in print and available to the academic community, this edition
was produced using digital reprint technology in a relatively short print run. This would
not have been attainable using traditional methods. Although the cover has been changed
from its original appearance, the text remains the same and all materials and methods
used still conform to the highest book-making standards.

Contents

Acknowledgments

The authors would like to thank Stephanie M. Lanz, Andrew Li, Steve Chu, and Preston Golson for their help in researching and writing this study.

Chapter 1

The Changing Nature of Critical Infrastructure Protection

There is nothing new about critical infrastructure protection. The U.S. carried out limited contingency planning to deal with threats to a number of its infrastructure facilities during the Cold War. These included key utilities such as power plants and grids, oil and gas pipelines, telecommunication, and critical facilities that affected the continuity of government. Most such U.S. efforts, however, were limited. While contingency planning did take place to deal with the threat posed by pro-Soviet "sleepers" or Russian covert attacks by forces such as the Spetsnaz, the damage such attacks could do was seen as only a peripheral part of the kind of damage that might occur in a nuclear exchange.

Nevertheless, these threats to America's critical infrastructure were never taken seriously enough during the Cold War to justify the funding of any major federal programs. Continuity of government and related facilities were the only forms of infrastructure protection to receive major funding in the context of a nuclear attack. Other than that, response relied largely on the existing law enforcement capabilities and those resources already required for dealing with accidents, weather, and acts of God. The threat posed by other perpetrators such as terrorists, extremists, criminals, and ideologically motivated individuals was seen as too limited to justify action beyond the self-protection measures taken by individual companies and institutions involved, and routine law enforcement. Even the most serious attempts at sabotage—usually by disgruntled employees—historically was in the "noise level" of the damage done by accidents, weather, and acts of God.

During the last two decades, however, the infrastructure of the American economy has fundamentally changed. It has steadily increased its reliance on its service sector and high technology economy and increasingly relies on computers, electronic data storage and transfers, and highly integrated communications networks. The result is a new form of critical infrastructure, one that is vulnerable to a new family of threats, loosely grouped together as information warfare.

THE PROBLEM OF EVOLVING TECHNOLOGY

This process of change is forcing the U.S. government, as well as civil and private sector users of information systems, to fundamentally reassess the role they must play in critical infrastructure protection. In the case of government, this process is forcing government agencies to act at a time when the infrastructure they are trying to protect is changing far more quickly than government can normally react. In many cases, "pre-computer" officials and managers must try to cope with a technology, economy, and society they no longer fully understand. The result is a "generation gap" of a kind that has not existed since the early 19th century and the peak periods of change during the industrial revolution.

There is no way to forecast precisely how this new infrastructure will evolve over even a period as short as a couple of years. Indeed, new generations of products are being released every six to nine months. Several things, however, are clear: Information systems are steadily becoming a more critical aspect of the American economy, government, and national security at every level.

These systems are increasingly being linked and integrated both on a national and global level and have already radically changed the way we do business. While physical damage to the nation's infrastructure remains a problem, information systems can be attacked electronically from anywhere in the world, posing a new kind of threat to both the nation's critical infrastructure and the American homeland.

THE UNCERTAIN BALANCE OF RISKS AND
NON-RISKS IN CYBER-ATTACKS

In fact, the problem of cyber-attacks has grown to such an extent that some predict an "electronic Waterloo" or an "electronic Pearl Harbor." It is far from clear that this level of potential damage from cyber-attack is likely or even possible. It is, however, at least a theoretical possibility. Resolving this very uncertainty is one of the most critical priorities in improving the U.S. effort in critical infrastructure protection. Many of the warnings regarding such dangers come from "experts" with little personal technical expertise, or who have a strong vested interest in either federal programs for cyber-defense or in commercial cyber-protection systems. There is no substantive unclassified analysis to support such broad claims of danger and vulnerability.

The Disconnect between Cyber-defense and Cyber-offense

There is also a clear disconnect between the efforts in the U.S. to plan offensive cyber-warfare and efforts at cyber-defense. Many defenders also assert that "technology 101" favors the attacker, prevents attribution, and makes counteroffense difficult or impossible. Some "attackers" and intelligence experts sharply question these views, and others see offense and defense as an ongoing duel whose outcome is unclear.

U.S. military and defense officials involved in information warfare and planning and executing cyber-war have divided views. Those directly involved in cyber-offense, however, generally seem to feel that carrying out a successful major cyber-attack is far more difficult than those outside the national security arena recognize. They do not minimize the risk of cyber-attacks, but they feel they will have limited impact and that many if not most critical systems are isolated, difficult to identify and enter in concerted attacks, and can be reconstituted within an acceptable time frame and cost.

This disconnect between defense and offense illustrates a basic problem underlying both any unclassified analysis of cyber-threats and their impact on homeland defense and a critical gap in the federal response to these threats:

- There is a clear need for a comprehensive annual net assessment of cyber-threats that combines an analysis of the threat that states can present in terms of cyber-warfare with the threats that foreign and domestic groups and non-state actors can present in terms of cyber-crime and cyber-terrorism. The sharp conceptual and analytic disconnects in analyzing and responding to cyber-warfare, cyber-terrorism, and cyber-crime, and the inability to establish a proper perspective as to the importance of each level of threat—and the required level of federal response, permeates U.S. government efforts and—as a result—the response of state and local authorities, the private sector, and non-governmental organizations.

- There is a clear need for some form of annual net technical assessment of the balance of offense and defense that can guide federal programs, and whose conclusions can be used to advise government, business, and NGOs.

Much of this work will involve some of the most sensitive areas of classified operations and technology in the U.S. government, and such a net assessment virtually has to be conducted within the national security community. At the same time, ways must be found to convincingly communicate the results to other federal government agencies, state and local governments, and to the private sector.

- There is a clear need for ongoing outside debate about the balance between offense and defense and to move beyond poorly supported assertions that can either over or understate the threat.

The Lack of Credible Risk and Vulnerability Assessments

Equally serious problems exist over how to estimate vulnerability, risk, and cost. Most of the estimates of the cost of cyber-crime and cracking, and the economic risk of cyber-attacks, seem to be little more than crude back of the envelope calculations with little or no credibility. Many, if not most, seem designed to grossly exaggerate the risk and cost to make a point.

These problems are compounded by the tendency to ignore the fact that ordinary crime and systems failures are an endemic reality in every aspect of government, business, and the nation's infrastructure. Storms, weather patterns, mechanical failures, and a host of other actuarial realities constantly "attack" the nation's critical infrastructure and the normal operations of government and business. Many of these events also lead to exaggerated estimates of loss and cost, which ignore the ability to recoup any losses over time.

There are major problems in identifying the point at which any successful attack would, in fact, be serious enough to justify federal intervention or really damage the nation's critical infrastructure in serious and lasting ways. From the perspective of any given business or NGO, a catastrophic attack on its information systems could be crippling or have massive consequences. However, from a national perspective, businesses and NGOs fail or suffer crippling damage for many reasons, and the nation has survived. Major temporary failures in the operation of communications systems, commerce, utility services, stock transactions, et cetera are an ongoing fact of life.

At the same time, the pressure to create steadily more complex systems can create chains of interlocking vulnerability that are very difficult to detect and predict. It can be argued that many who assess cyber-vulnerability fail to evaluate the ongoing evolution of defensive efforts in reaction to the constant pressure from crackers and cyber-criminals.

Yet, it can be argued that models do not exist for analyzing complex patterns of vulnerability to more sophisticated patterns of attack. The limited number of federal tests and exercises that have attempted to measure vulnerability to date raise real questions about such vulnerabilities, although some suffer from a structure that exercises technical assumptions rather than measuring actual vulnerability.

This again supports the need for an annual net technical assessment to establish the actual state of vulnerability in government and the private sector, and the areas where federal intervention may really be justified in terms of homeland defense. This will present major technical challenges, but it is clearly necessary because at present there seems to be no real basis for prioritizing federal efforts or guiding state and local governments and the private sector.

The lack of such vulnerability assessments also tends to favor those who believe in boosting defense against ongoing or known methods of cyber-attack, rather than solutions based on designing less vulnerable systems. This defensive posture focuses on increasing the isolation of systems from attack, adding measures to reconstitute systems, providing more capable back-up systems and alternatives, and ameliorating attacks or failures once they occur. Specifically addressing all of these options should be a critical aspect of such a vulnerability assessment.

GOVERNMENTAL AND PRIVATE SECTOR EFFORTS TO RESPOND

In spite of these problems, the federal government is making real progress in its efforts to defend the nation's changing critical infrastructure and is steadily improving its coordination with state and local governments as well as the private sector. It has developed new policies, new organizational approaches, and has completed its first national plan. Total funding for critical infrastructure protection has risen from $1.14 billion in FY1998 to $2.03 billion in FY2001, and the U.S. is steadily improving its intelligence and law enforcement efforts.

The private sector is learning how to cope with the fact that its growing dependence on constantly evolving, cutting-edge information systems creates new vulnerabilities, new patterns of crime, and new risks of sabotage. As the primary user of information systems, it is still learning how to strike a cost-effective balance between securing its cyber and information systems and business efficiency. Businesses and NGOs are forced to constantly learn and adapt, however, by the constant flood of efforts to crack their systems. At the same time, insurance companies and regulators are beginning to develop standards for performance and to realize that even the best systems cannot avoid the loss of billions of dollars a year.

Much of the U.S. government reaction to the threat to both government and private sector vulnerabilities is preliminary and lags behind the high rate of change. There are fundamental issues that must be resolved. Almost inevitably, the definition of critical infrastructure protection used by different departments and agencies tends to vary according to their mission and responsibility. In many cases, it includes both the traditional definitions of infrastructure and information systems. In other cases, protection includes any incident requiring federal intervention from natural disasters to war, although most agencies concentrate on their day-to-day civil missions in areas like law enforcement and coping with natural disasters.

It is clear that the federal government must preserve its national security functions and prepare for attacks by foreign governments and terrorists and support law enforcement. What is not clear, however, is how vulnerability should be measured; what linkage exists between given vulnerabilities; what the probability of given forms of attack are; and where the role of the federal government ends and that of the state and local governments and the private sector begins.

One key challenge is obvious and needs urgent federal action. The federal government must make a clear determination of what kind of threats can be dealt with as cyber-crime or low-level penetrations, and what threats merit serious federal attention.

In the case of attacks involving foreign governments and major foreign terrorists and extremist movements, it is not clear what laws apply. What constitutes an act of war in the networked environment and what kind of counterattack or offensive operations are justified are poorly defined. Cyber-war and cyber-terrorism are still in their infancy, making such definitions and response levels harder to formulate. During Kosovo, the U.S. found that it did not have a clear basis in law for deciding how to retaliate against computer attacks by Serbia. Moreover, a major debate emerged between the information warfare community, which generally favored counterattacks on Serbia, and the intelligence community, which saw such attacks as threatening its intelligence collection capabilities. These problems were compounded by the fact that the role of third nations or "neutrals" in preventing the use of their cyber-facilities and information systems was not clear. In fact, even allies participating in the NATO operations in Kosovo had no basis for deciding what actions they could take to limit the use of relatively unsophisticated enabling technologies like cellular phones and laptops.

For some time to come, the U.S. is going to have to treat each new case as precedent setting in the international law and conflict arena because attacks that are not linked to physical conflict or traditional forms of war are difficult to categorize. It is not clear that they should be recognized as forms of conflict. Furthermore, retaliation becomes a problem because some interpret the present rules of engagement as forbidding any response that might produce collateral damage affecting actors other than those directly engaged in the conflict. The problem is that because there is no blueprint of the Internet—indeed most companies or institutions would be hard put to produce a comprehensive plan of their own networks much less their interconnections—it is very difficult to gauge what the unintended consequences of a cyber-attack would be. There is no way to know what the collateral damage would be or if an attack would end up having a boomerang effect. The remediation work carried out to deal with Y2K did a lot to map out interconnections between companies and their partners. However, the system changes so rapidly that if these plans are not regularly updated the progress made in understanding the interrelationships between systems made during Y2K will soon be lost.

The responsibility of friendly and neutral foreign governments to aid the U.S. is unclear, as is the level of force with which the U.S. might actively retaliate if foreign governments do not take effective action. Attacks linked to high levels of more conventional forms of attack on the American homeland could greatly complicate U.S. defense and response against other emerging threats like CBRN attacks. For credible deterrence, the U.S. will have to create a clear retaliatory or offensive plan, be able to implement it convincingly, communicate it to attackers, and target and attack actual attacks in nearly real time. This will be extremely difficult due to the uncertainty of detecting the attacker as well as the ambiguity of when a cyber-attack is termed an act of war, and exacerbated by the poorly defined allocation of responsibility for response that creates an unclear chain of command. Simple bureaucratic inertia also hinders the normal command structure from executing a timely response when faced with an attack that can last only seconds or minutes.

There are equally serious and complicated issues in dealing with private individuals and criminals who engage in cyber-attacks targeting the U.S. both domestically and internationally. The U.S. is developing a body of law for seeking out and prosecuting domestic cyber-criminals and other "attackers" at both the federal and state level. This effort is hampered by the need to strike a very delicate balance between law enforcement activities and civil rights. This is especially true when dealing with the "hobbyist"-like character of crackers and hackers that present major problems to the intelligence community. Also, major problems still exist when trying to determine civil and criminal responsibility of the private sector for ensuring that adequate protection and defense measures are in place.

Cyber-crime creates new jurisdictional and data sharing problems, particularly when both domestic and foreign criminals are involved, calling for new levels of technical expertise at virtually every level. There already are a large number of hackers, crackers, and criminals who not only "attack" systems inside the U.S., but also target U.S. interests overseas. Traditional law enforcement, however, stops at the national borders whereas cyber-crime does not. The perpetrators can be anywhere in the world and unless there is international cooperation it is very difficult to arrest and prosecute the attacker. Unfortunately, in most countries, there is no clear basis in law for prosecuting cyber-criminals and no basis for extradition. Furthermore, crackers and hackers can escalate into full fledged cyber-terrorists who may have few of the traditional motivating interests that allow law enforcement and intelligence officials to identify and track small non-state actors.

Computer attacks carried out by well-organized terrorist/extremist groups, and foreign governments and their proxies, are likely to pose a far more serious threat than individual criminals because their motive is destruction and not profit. There is also the added risk that they will use their cyber-attack capabilities to disrupt responses or inflict additional damage if they ever are willing to take the risk of a missile or CBRN attack on the U.S. With time, ingenuity, and modest financial backing, even a small group of skilled attackers might be able to cause serious damage to the critical infrastructure. This risk was clearly demonstrated by "Eligible Receiver," an exercise carried out at the request of the Joint Chiefs of Staff.

Two things are clear:

- First, the bulk of defensive action must take place at a time when there already is a near-constant flow of attacks on the nation's information systems. Since most of the critical infrastructures are owned and operated by the private sector, the users and providers must supply virtually all of the defense and response capability themselves. The federal government can, at most, play a limited role through law enforcement, prepare to deal with major terrorist and/or military forms of information warfare, and respond to truly severe attacks on the nation's infrastructure.

- Second, the technology of electronic offense and defense is so complex and is changing so quickly that all defensive efforts must constantly evolve and change rather than play catch-up. This also means that the process for appropriations and allocation of funds needs to be revisited so that necessary moneys can be released in a timely manner. The federal government must accept the reality that this is a problem unlike any it has ever dealt with before. Neither the best-laid plans nor the most developed capabilities can anticipate the real nature of major cyber-terrorism or provide advanced notice of a full-scale cyber-war. The government may try, but ultimately it will be its ability to respond and adapt in real time that will be at least as critical as its ability to anticipate the future.

These problems again highlight the need to find the dividing line between the problems and losses that are an inevitable result of the growing dependence on computers and information systems, and those that create the need for federal action. It seems likely that some 95% of all the problems and challenges posed by criminals, crackers, and hackers will have to be dealt with in the same way damage from other criminal activities are reduced. Use of alarms and passive defenses, law enforcement activity can reduce costs, and some damage can reasonably be treated as normal actuarial losses and the "cost of doing business."

The problem for homeland defense lies with the other cases, where deliberate foreign, terrorist, extremist, criminal cracker, and hacker attacks pose a serious threat to the national interest which can escalate from attacks on critical services and sectors of the economy to open warfare. In these cases, the federal government and state and local authorities must develop cost-effective deterrence, defense, counterattack, amelioration, repair, and compensation measures.

Chapter 2

Threat Assessment

The U.S. government has made progress in many aspects of its efforts to assess the cyber-threat and in improving its capabilities in cyber-intelligence. As is the case with other evolving threats, however, there are major uncertainties that even the best organized effort can not overcome. The world is changing rapidly, and there is no consensus on which way it will develop, the nature of future vulnerabilities, and the types of attacks that will exploit these vulnerabilities.

There is nothing theoretical about the prospect of low-level attacks. Cyber-crime has grown in almost direct proportion to the growth in dependence on information systems, reflecting an inevitable linkage between crime and technological change. It does not help that tools that are needed to carry out attacks are readily available to anybody via the Internet. At one point, Interpol estimated that there were as many as 30,000 web sites that provided some form of automated hacking tools—"hacking made easy." As a result, such attacks have also become a "sport" of sorts. Nearly every aspect of American computer networks are under continuous "attack," although the motive behind such attacks is often little more than an attempt to prove that a system can be broken into or exploited.[1]

Unfortunately, the seemingly frightening statistics on such attacks—and the certainty that many more are unrecorded—is difficult to correlate with the importance and seriousness of such attacks. In most cases, such attacks are virtually meaningless. In a small minority of cases they can have serious consequences. At present, there is no way of establishing the importance of most attacks, and further problems also exist because changes in reporting methods often produce major increases in the number of reported incidents that appear to be trends but are not really based on the same counting procedures. The sheer mass of data in question makes it difficult for defenders to keep detailed long-term network logs for later comparative analysis.

The constant flood of "horror" stories about low-level cyber-attacks must be kept in careful perspective. There is a natural bias toward exaggerating the importance of such attacks on the part of those who make a living out of defending against such attacks. There have been many estimates of the "cost" of hacking, cyber-crime, and petty cyber-terrorism that produce grossly exaggerated estimates of its impact on business and which do so using methods of estimating cost that range from inadequate to absurd. Like figures on shoplifting, figures on total cyber-hits and penetrations can be far more alarming than serious. Crime, vandalism, and low-level terrorism will always expand along with changes in the economy, society, and structure of government. They will also expand far more quickly when the pace of changes in the economy, society, and structure of government is rapid. Government and the private sector will have to learn to live with this level of attacks, and is already learning to do so.

The problem for homeland and defense and critical infrastructure protection is that far more serious threats are possible, if not probable. Hostile states and terrorists have learned to both exploit and attack networks, computers, data storage, and other information systems. Experts note that terrorists and extremists are increasingly using the Internet for communication and propaganda purposes; to raise funds and manage their finances; and are launching attacks on government systems around the world.[2] Some groups also seem to be involved in cyber-crime such as identity theft in order to aid their funding and acquisition goals. As a result, such movements are developing skills they may use far more aggressively in the future.

Foreign governments are learning how to launch forms of information warfare that go far beyond the electronic warfare envisaged during the Cold War. Nowadays, not only military systems but financial, corporate, civil government, media, NGO, or educational information systems that connected to the outside world can become a target. Some governments, like China, have made cyber-warfare a critical part of their military doctrine, in part to help counter the advantage the U.S. has in conventional and nuclear warfighting capability. As a result, cyber-warfare is becoming a critical element of asymmetric warfare, and nations hostile to the U.S. are developing plans and capabilities to use it either as a single form of attack or in concert with other forms of asymmetric warfare.

THE PRESIDENT'S COMMISSION ON CRITICAL INFRASTRUCTURE PROTECTION CHARACTERIZATION OF THE THREAT

The federal government and private organizations have developed a number of reports on the nature and scale of the threat. In 1997, President Clinton set up a President's Commission on Critical Infrastructure Protection. This commission made one of the first major efforts to assess the threat. Its recommendations also played a crucial role in shaping U.S. understanding of the new vulnerabilities it faces as part of the information age. The commission's report stated that cyber-attacks could occur on many different levels and identified five major types of possible attacks:

- A cyber-attack on the specific database of an owner/operator
- A cyber-attack for the purpose of gaining access to a network
- A cyber-attack for the purpose of espionage
- A cyber-attack for the purpose of shutting down service
- A cyber-attack for the purpose of introducing harmful instructions.[3]

Although these five forms of attack do not distinguish between attacks on civil capabilities in the U.S. and attacks in support of military operations, the commission also made the following general observations about possible forms of attack, and the problems in characterizing them.[4]

If the basic cyber-attack tools are common across the spectrum, what may distinguish recreational hackers from information warriors (IN) is *organization.* Said another way, an IW attack on the U.S. infrastructure may be little more than a series of hacker attacks, conducted against a carefully chosen and thoroughly reconnoitered targets, synchronized in time, to accomplish specific purposes.

For an adversary willing to take greater risk, cyber-attacks could be combined with physical attacks against facilities or against human targets in an effort to paralyze a large segment of society, damage our capability to respond to incidents (by disabling the 911 system of emergency communications, for example), hamper our ability to deploy conventional military forces, and otherwise limit the freedom of action of our national leadership. . . .

The chances of immediately discovering that a concerted cyber-attack is in progress are today even slimmer. Computer intrusions do not announce their presence the way a bomb does. Depending on the skill of the intruder and the technology and training available on their own system administrators, individual companies whose networks are penetrated may or may not detect an intrusion. Intrusions that are discovered may or may not be reported to law enforcement authorities, who may or may not have the resources to investigate them and conclude whether they are the work of an insider, a hacker, a criminal, or someone truly bent on harming the infrastructure. It sometimes takes months, even years, to determine the significance of individual computer attacks. . . .

The problems the commission raised in assessing cyber-threats and vulnerability are as valid today as they were in 1997. It is important to note, however, that the commission did not set forth proposals to improve the assessment of vulnerability, the quality of reporting on the threat, or ways to assess the importance of given forms of attack. This is a continuing problem in federal efforts to cope with the new threat to the U.S. homeland.

THE NATIONAL INFRASTRUCTURE PROTECTION CENTER'S (NIPC) VIEW OF THE THREAT

There are some federal statistics on the scale of threat. As a result of PDD-63, the FBI established the National Infrastructure Protection Center (NIPC) located at FBI headquarters and regional computer intrusion squads located in selected offices throughout the U.S. The NIPC has several functions. It attempts to track the expanding number of instances in which criminals have targeted major components of information and economic infrastructure systems; it is a joint partnership among federal agencies and private industry; and it is designed to serve as the government's lead mechanism for preventing and responding to cyber-attacks on the nation's infrastructures. These infrastructures include telecommunications, energy, transportation, banking and finance, emergency services, and government operations.

The mission of regional computer intrusion squads is to investigate violations of the Computer Fraud and Abuse Act (Title 8, Section 1030), including intrusions to public switched networks, major computer network intrusions, privacy violations, industrial espionage, pirated computer software, and other crimes

These efforts have enabled NIPC to develop an annual report that tries to quantify the threat. According to a 1999 year-end incident activity summary by its FedCIRC (Federal Computer Incident Response Capability), a total of 580 incidents were reported to FedCIRC, involving 1,496,268 hosts. The majority of these types of incidents were reconnaissance in nature (40%—233), attempts to gain root[5] access (18%—110) and information requests (14%—79). Out of the rest of the incidents virus and denial of service attacks accounted for 10% (5% each). These incidents are described by type in Table 2.1.

Such counts do not provide a picture of the importance of such attacks, even when successful, and have severe statistical uncertainty. The Director of the National Infrastructure Protection Center (NIPC),

Table 2.1
Summary FedCIRC (Federal Computer Incident Response Capability) Survey of Incident Activity in 1999 (Summary of Incident Types)

Count	Percentage	Type
233	40%	Reconnaissance
110	18%	Root compromise
79	14%	Information request
45	7%	Unknown
45	7%	Known unsuccessful attack
33	5%	Virus
33	5%	Denial of Service
23	3%	User Compromise
14	2%	Misuse of resources
5	<1%	Deception
4	<1%	False Alarm

Note: This information has been provided to convey a general impression of the variety of intruder activity reported to us. Incident statistics are presented only after we have analyzed and categorized them. They should not be interpreted as a chronological record of intruder activities. More than one activity type can be assigned to an incident. Complex incidents may involve more intruder activities than are explicitly identified. Incident details may not be 100% complete or contain the same level of detail for every incident. Host and site counts are approximate and may not reflect the exact number of hosts involved in the incident. Because some incident reports may be closed and then reopened again at a later date, the totals given in this year-end report may differ slightly from the sums of the numbers listed in the previous twelve monthly reports.

Source: "FedCIRC Incident Activity Summary for 1999" http:// www2.fedcirc.gov/stats/1999.html accessed 07/07/00.

Michael A. Vatis, has, however, given testimony that helps put these numbers in context and provides a broader assessment of the threats to U.S. information security.[6] Vatis made the following key points:[7]

- According to former Deputy Secretary of Defense John Hamre the DoD is "detecting 80 to 100 [potential hacking] events daily."
- Foreign nations are developing information warfare programs. Chinese military officers published a book calling for the use of unconventional measures such as the use of computer viruses as a way to attack the United States' technological dominance.[8] There were concerted attempts by hackers sympathetic to Yugoslavia to attack NATO Web servers.
- Foreign intelligence services use cyberspace to achieve information-gathering objectives. The "Cuckoo's Egg" case was an instance in which West German hackers hacked into military, scientific, and industrial computers of the U.S., Western Europe, and Japan between 1986 and 1989, stealing passwords and programs which they sold to the USSR.
- Terrorists actively use the Internet to spread propaganda, raise funds, and formulate plans securely through communication technology. He cited the examples such as that of the World Trade Center bombing "mastermind" Ramzi Yousef storing detail encrypted plans to destroy U.S. airliners on his laptop, incidents in Sri Lanka of a group which calls itself the "Internet Black Tigers" attacking Sri Lankan government servers through "denial of service" attacks, and other discovered cyber-terrorism plots in Mexico and Japan as evidence of the growing threat such information security issues pose.
- Ongoing threats are posed by cyber-criminals, recreational hackers, virus writers, and "hactivists."

Vatis went on to provide a more detailed picture of the threat which provides one of the best overviews to date of the emerging threat to the nation's critical infrastructure.[9]

Spectrum of Threats

The news media is filled with examples of intrusions into government and private sector computer networks. Politically motivated hackers have been attacking numerous U.S. Government Web sites, including the Senate's. Deputy Secretary of Defense John Hamre reported in February that DoD is "detecting 80 to 100 [potential hacking] events daily." We have had several damaging computer viruses this year, including the Melissa Macro Virus, the Explorer Zip Worm, and the CIH (Chernobyl) Virus. Computer Economics, Inc., a California firm, estimates that damage in the first two quarters of 1999 from viruses has topped $7 billion. The FBI's caseload for computer hacking and network intrusion cases has doubled each of the last two years. Currently we have over 800 pending investigations. In its 1999 survey, the Computer Security Institute estimated the total financial losses by the 163 businesses it surveyed from computer security breaches at $123.7 million. This includes everything from theft of proprietary data to denial of service on networks. E-commerce has become so important that firms, including Sedgwick Group PLC (in cooperation with IBM), Lloyds of London, and Network Risk Management Services, are now offering "hacker insurance."

Sensitive Intrusions

In the past few years we have seen a series of intrusions into numerous Department of Defense computer networks as well as networks of other federal agencies, universities, and private sector entities. Intruders have successfully accessed U.S. Government networks and took large amounts of unclassified but sensitive information. In investigating these cases, the NIPC has been coordinating with FBI field offices, the Department of Defense, and other government agencies, as circumstances require. But it is important that Congress and the American public understand the very real threat that we are facing in the cyber-realm, not just in the future, but now.

Information Warfare

Perhaps the greatest potential threat to our national security is the prospect of "information warfare" by foreign militaries against our critical infrastructures. We know that several foreign nations are already developing information warfare doctrine, programs, and capabilities for use against each other and the U.S. or other nations. Foreign nations are developing information warfare programs because they see that they cannot defeat the U.S. in a head-to-head military encounter and they believe that information operations are a way to strike at what they perceive as America's Achilles' heel—our reliance on information technology to control critical government and private sector systems. For example, two Chinese military officers recently published a book that called for the use of unconventional measures, including the propagation of computer viruses, to counterbalance the military power of the U.S. In addition, during the recent conflict in Yugoslavia, hackers sympathetic to Serbia electronically "ping" attacked NATO Web servers. And Russian as well as other individuals supporting the Serbs attacked Web sites in NATO countries, including the U.S., using virus-infected e-mail and hacking attempts. Over 100 entities in the U.S. received these e-mails. Several British organizations lost files and databases. These attacks did not cause any disruption of the military effort, and the attacked entities quickly recovered. But such attacks are portents of much more serious attacks that we can expect foreign adversaries to attempt in future conflicts.

Foreign Intelligence Services

Foreign intelligence services have adapted to using cyber-tools as part of their information gathering and espionage tradecraft. In a case dubbed "the Cuckoo's Egg," between 1986 and 1989 a ring of West German hackers penetrated numerous military, scientific, and industry computers in the U.S., Western Europe, and Japan, stealing passwords, programs, and other information which they sold to the Soviet KGB. Significantly, this was over a decade ago—ancient history in Internet years. While I cannot go into specifics about the situation today in an open hearing, it is clear that foreign intelligence services increasingly view computer intrusions as a useful tool for acquiring sensitive U.S. government and private sector information.

Terrorists

Terrorists are known to use information technology and the Internet to formulate plans, raise funds, spread propaganda, and to communicate securely. For example, convicted terrorist Ramzi Yousef, the mastermind of the World Trade Center bombing, stored detailed plans to destroy U.S. airliners on encrypted files on his laptop computer. Moreover, some groups have already used cyber-attacks to inflict damage on their enemies' information systems. For example, a group calling itself the Internet Black Tigers conducted a successful "denial of service" attack on servers of Sri Lankan government embassies. Italian sympathizers of the Mexican Zapatista rebels attacked Web pages of Mexican financial institutions. And a Canadian government report indicates that the Irish Republican Army has considered the use of information operations against British interests. We are also concerned that Aum Shinrikyo, which launched the deadly Sarin gas attack in the Tokyo subway system, could use its growing expertise in computer manufacturing and Internet technology to develop "cyber-terrorism" weapons for use against Japanese and U.S. interests. Thus while we have yet to see a significant instance of "cyber-terrorism" with widespread disruption of critical infrastructures, all of these facts portend the use of cyber-attacks by terrorists to cause pain to targeted governments or civilian populations by disrupting critical systems.

Criminal Groups

We are also beginning to see the increased use of cyber-intrusions by criminal groups who attack systems for purposes of monetary gain. For example, in 1994, the U.S. Secret Service uncovered a $50 million phone card scam that abused the accounts of AT&T, MCI, and Sprint customers. In addition, in 1994–95 an organized crime group headquartered in St. Petersburg, Russia, transferred $10.4 million from Citibank into accounts all over the world. After surveillance and investigation by the FBI's New York field office, all but $400,000 of the funds were recovered. In another case, Carlos Felipe Salgado, Jr. gained unauthorized access to several Internet service providers in California and stole 100,000 credit card numbers with a combined limit of over $1 billion. The FBI arrested him in the San Francisco International Airport when he tried to sell the credit card numbers to a cooperating witness for $260,000. With the expansion of electronic commerce, we expect to see an increase in hacking by organized crime as the new frontier for large-scale theft.

Just two weeks ago, two members of a group dubbed the "phonemasters" were sentenced after their conviction for theft and possession of unauthorized access devices (18 USC §1029) and unauthorized access to a federal interest computer (18 USC §1030). The "phonemasters" are an international group of criminals who penetrated the computer systems of MCI, Sprint, AT&T, Equifax, and even the FBI's National Crime Information Center (NCIC). Under judicially approved electronic surveillance orders, the FBI's Dallas field office made use of new data intercept technology to monitor the calling activity and modem pulses of one of the suspects, Calvin Cantrell. Mr. Cantrell downloaded thousands of Sprint calling card numbers, which he sold to a Canadian individual, who passed them on to someone in Ohio. These numbers made their way to an individual in Switzerland and eventually ended up in the hands of organized crime groups in Italy. Mr. Cantrell was sentenced to two years as a result of his guilty plea, while one of his associates, Cory Lindsay, was sentenced to 41 months.

The "phonemasters" activities should serve as a wake up call for corporate security. Their methods included "dumpster diving" to gather old phone books and technical manuals for systems. They then used this information to trick employees into giving up their logon and password information. The group then used this information to break into victim systems. It is important to remember that often "cyber-crimes" are facilitated by old-fashioned guile, such as calling employees and tricking them into giving up passwords. Good "cyber-security" practices must therefore address personnel security and "social engineering" in addition to instituting electronic security measures.

Virus Writers

Virus writers are posing an increasingly serious threat to networks and systems worldwide. As noted above, we have had several damaging computer viruses this year, including the Melissa Macro Virus, the Explore.Zip worm, and the CIH (Chernobyl) Virus. The NIPC frequently sends out warnings regarding particularly dangerous viruses.

Earlier this year, we reacted quickly to the spread of the Melissa Macro Virus. While there are dozens of viruses released every day, the speedy propagation of Melissa and its effects on networks caused us great concern. Within hours of learning about the virus on Friday, March 26, 1999, we had coordinated with key cyber-response components of DoD and the

Computer Emergency Response Team (CERT) at Carnegie-Mellon University. Our Watch operation went into 24-hour posture and sent out warning messages to federal agencies, state and local law enforcement, FBI field offices, and the private sector. Because the virus affected systems throughout the public, we also took the unusual step of issuing a public warning through the FBI's Public Affairs Office and on our Web site. These steps helped mitigate the damage by alerting computer users of the virus and of protective steps they could take.

On the investigative side, the NIPC acted as a central point of contact for the field offices who worked leads on the case. A tip received by the New Jersey State Police from America Online, and their follow-up investigation with the FBI's Newark field office, led to the April 1, 1999 arrest of David L. Smith. Search warrants were executed in New Jersey by the New Jersey State Police and FBI Special Agents from the Newark field office.

Earlier this year we saw reports on the Suppl Word Macro virus, the toadie.exe virus, and the W97M/Thurs.A (or Thursday) virus. This last virus has already infected over 5,000 machines, according to news reports, and deletes files on victims' hard drives. The payload of the virus is triggered on 12-13 and disables the macro virus protection in Word 97. We are also concerned with the propagation of a Trojan Horse called Back Orifice 2000, which allows malicious actors to monitor or tamper with computers undetected by the users.

Virus writers are not often broken out as a threat category, and yet they often do more damage to networks than hackers do. The prevalence of computer viruses reminds us that we all have to be very careful about the attachments we open and we all must be sure to keep our anti-virus software up-to-date.

Hactivism

Recently we have seen a rise in what has been dubbed "hacktivism"— politically motivated attacks on publicly accessible Web pages or e-mail servers. These groups and individuals overload e-mail servers and hack into Web sites to send a political message. While these attacks generally have not altered operating systems or networks, they still damage services and deny the public access to Web sites containing valuable information and infringe on others' right to communicate. One such group is called the "Electronic Disturbance Theater," which promotes civil disobedience on-line in support of its political agenda regarding the Zapatista movement in Mexico and other issues. This past spring they called for worldwide electronic civil disobedience and have taken what they term "protest actions" against White House and Department of Defense servers. Supporters of Kevin Mitnick, recently convicted of numerous computer security offenses, hacked into the Senate Web page and defaced it in May and June of this past year. The Internet has enabled new forms of political gathering and information sharing for those who want to advance social causes; that is good for our democracy. But illegal activities that disrupt e-mail servers, deface Web sites, and prevent the public from accessing information on U.S. government and private sector Web sites should be regarded as criminal acts that deny others their First Amendment rights to communicate rather than as an acceptable form of protest.

"Recreational" Hackers

Virtually every day we see a report about "recreational hackers," or "crackers," who crack into networks for the thrill of the challenge or for bragging rights in the hacker community. While remote cracking once required a fair amount of skill or computer knowledge, the recreational hacker can now download attack scripts and protocols from the World Wide Web and launch them against victim sites. Thus while attack tools have become more sophisticated, they have also become easier to use.

These types of hacks are very numerous and may appear on their face to be benign. But they can have serious consequences. A well-known example of this involved a juvenile who hacked into the NYNEX (now Bell Atlantic) telephone system that serviced the Worcester, Massachusetts area using his personal computer and modem. The hacker shut down telephone service to 600 customers in the local community. The resulting disruption affected all local police and fire 911 services as well as the ability of incoming aircraft to activate the runway lights at the Worcester airport. Telephone service was out at the airport tower for six hours. The U.S. Secret Service investigation of this case also brought to light vulnerability in 22,000 telephone switches nationwide that could be taken down with four keystrokes. Because he was a juvenile, however, the hacker was sentenced to only two years probation and 250 hours of community service, and was forced to forfeit the computer equipment used to hack into the phone system and reimburse the phone company for $5,000. This case demonstrated that an attack against our critical communications hubs can have cascading effects on several infrastructures. In this case, transportation, emergency services, and telecommunications were disrupted. It also showed that widespread disruption could be caused by a single person from his or her home computer.

Insider Threat

The disgruntled insider is a principal source of computer crimes. Insiders do not need a great deal of knowledge about computer intrusions because their knowledge of victim systems often allows them to gain unrestricted access to cause damage to the system or to steal system data. The 1999 Computer Security Institute/FBI report notes that 55% of respondents reported malicious activity by insiders.

There are many cases in the public domain involving disgruntled insiders. For example, Shakuntla Devi Singla used her insider knowledge and another employee's password and logon identification to delete data from a U.S. Coast Guard personnel database system. It took 115 agency employees over 1800 hours to recover and reenter the lost data. Ms. Singla was convicted and sentenced to five months in prison, five months home detention, and ordered to pay $35,000 in restitution.

In another case, a former Forbes employee named George Parente hacked into Forbes' systems using another employee's password and login identification and crashed over half of Forbes' computer network servers and erased all of the data on each of the crashed services. The data could not be restored. The losses to Forbes were reportedly over $100,000.

Identifying the Intruder

One major difficulty that distinguishes cyber-threats from physical threats is determining who is attacking your system, why, how, and from where. This difficulty stems from the ease with which individuals can hide or disguise their tracks by manipulating logs and directing their attacks through networks in many countries before hitting their ultimate target. The now well-known "Solar Sunrise" case illustrates this point. Solar Sunrise was a multi-agency investigation (which occurred while the NIPC was being established) of intrusions into more than 500 military, civilian, government, and private sector computer systems in the U.S., during February and March 1998. The intrusions occurred during the build-up of U.S. military personnel in the Persian Gulf in response to tension with Iraq over United Nations weapons inspections. The intruders penetrated at least 200 unclassified U.S. military computer systems, including seven Air Force bases and four Navy installations, Department of Energy National Laboratories, NASA sites, and university sites. Agencies involved in the investigation included the FBI, DoD, NASA, Defense Information Systems Agency, AFOSI, and the Department of Justice.

The timing of the intrusions and links to some Internet service providers in the Gulf region caused many to believe that Iraq was behind the intrusions. The investigation, however, revealed that two juveniles in Cloverdale, California and several individuals in Israel were the culprits. Solar Sunrise thus demonstrated to the interagency community how difficult it is to identify an intruder until facts are gathered in an investigation and why assumptions cannot be made until sufficient facts are available. It also vividly demonstrated the vulnerabilities that exist in our networks; if these individuals were able to assume "root access" to DoD systems, it is not difficult to imagine what hostile adversaries with greater skills and resources would be able to do. Finally, Solar Sunrise demonstrated the need for interagency coordination by the NIPC.

It is striking that Vatis did not attempt to assess the scale of the growing threat of cyber-warfare and the activities of foreign governments in preparing for such conflicts. It must also be stressed that that the NPIC and FedCIRC data not only do not attempt to cost incidents or estimate their seriousness, they make no effort to trace their motive and ultimate national origin. This again illustrates the problems inherent in knowing how many attempts took place at an attack or characterizing attacks. At this point in time, many attacks go undetected or unreported. The reason for this can range from systems administrators not being able to detect an attack to the lack of security culture within the government and private sector. Also, reasons for not reporting can be anything from not knowing where or to whom to report, fear of loss of customer confidence, or simple embarrassment.

It is also unclear how many attacks are successful and how many successful attacks are detected and properly characterized. In fact, many such statistics are virtually useless in measuring the need and priorities for cyber-defense and critical infrastructure protection. They may dramatize the problem, but they also exaggerate one aspect of its importance while doing nothing to communicate levels of damage, cost, and risk, or providing context. This is a fatal, and increasingly inexcusable, flaw in such reporting. Cyber-intelligence is a new and emerging art form even when it must deal largely with levels of attack limited to hackers, crackers, criminals, and the occasional extremist or activist. These problems could be vastly greater in the event of cyber-terrorism or cyber-war.

INTELLIGENCE COMMUNITY ASSESSMENTS OF THE THREAT

U.S. intelligence community estimates of the threat seem to divide into assessments that focus on the ongoing threat of cyber-terrorism and cyber-crime and assessments that focus on the new and more serious threats that may emerge in the future. Both types of assessment help illustrate the problems the U.S. must deal with, as well as some of the limitations in its current approach to assessing the problem.

CIA Testimony on the Threat

Some of the best unclassified intelligence assessment of the threat is contained in the testimony of CIA Information Operations Issue Manager John A. Serabian Jr. before the Joint Economic Committee on Cyber Threats to the U.S. Economy. Like Vatis, Serabian did draw attention to the general threat posed by emerging nation-state cyber-warfare programs as well as the threat posed by terrorist and non-state actors, but did not provide any clear perspective as to how to prioritize such threats or measure their importance.[10]

Introduction

The Director of Central Intelligence, George Tenet, earlier this month testified before the Senate Select Committee on Intelligence in his annual worldwide threat briefing that the foreign cyber-threat is one of the key transnational issues that we face as a nation. In that testimony he noted that the U.S. is increasingly dependent on ". . . the unimpeded and secure flow of technology." Any adversary, foreign or domestic, that develops the ability to interrupt that flow ". . . will have the potential to weaken us dramatically or even render us helpless." The recent e-commerce attacks underscore this point. Whatever their motivation, the attackers have taken the threat out of the realm of the abstract and made it real.

The DCI in his testimony emphasized that ". . . as in so many areas in this technological age, we are truly in a race with technology itself." A major challenge in the next decade will be to find ways to defend our infrastructure and protect our commerce while maintaining an open society.

We cannot do all of these things simultaneously without a common understanding of the threat. Providing that understanding is and will remain a major thrust of the CIA and the intelligence community for years to come.

In this hearing today, Mr. Chairman, I hope to provide you with a further appreciation for the growing seriousness and significance of the emerging threat to our information systems. I want to emphasize our need to evaluate this threat across the full spectrum of state and non-state actors, recognizing that proliferation of malicious capabilities exists at every level and across an equally broad range of potential targets.

In light of the sophistication of many other countries and non-state actors in programming and Internet usage, the threat to our information systems has to be viewed as a factor requiring considerable attention by every agency of government.

Community Involvement

Let me emphasize that CIA involvement in protecting our information infrastructure extends not just to cooperation with others within the intelligence community, but to participating with most of the other stakeholders in protecting our nation's infrastructure systems, across government agencies, and throughout the private sector. In particular, the CIA has provided a range of support to the National Infrastructure Protection Center (NIPC) at the FBI since its inception. The CIA also disseminates cyber-threat assessments to the NIPC. The CIA also has provided the NIPC with technical and analytic support. In addition, the CIA has collaborated with NIPC and others in the U.S. intelligence community to develop and present outreach briefings on foreign cyber-threats to key infrastructure sector stakeholders, including elements of the private sector.

Threat

Let me take a moment to frame the problem in terms of "Who" constitutes a potential attacker; "What" motivates a cyber-attack; and "Why" this threat is so different from others we face.

Who would consider attacking our nation's information systems? Given the availability of sophisticated technology and the seemingly limited investment required, potential attackers can include national intelligence and military organizations, terrorists, criminals, industrial competitors, hackers, and disgruntled or disloyal insiders. Each of these potential adversaries is motivated by unique objectives, has various degrees of technical expertise and targeted access, and can tolerate different levels of risk.

What motivates an attack against the U.S. information infrastructure? There are any number of incentives, including economic, industrial, and military rationales. By way of example: Trillions of dollars in financial transactions and commerce move over a medium with minimal protection and only sporadic law enforcement, a structure that is the most complex the world has ever known. Increasing quantities of intellectual property reside on networked systems; and opportunities abound to disrupt military effectiveness and public safety while maintaining the elements of surprise and anonymity.

A Different Kind of Threat

Why is this threat so insidious and different? We have spent years building an information infrastructure that is interoperable, easy to access, and easy to use. Attributes like openness and ease of connectivity which promote efficiency and expeditious customer service are the same ones that now make the system vulnerable to attacks against automated information systems.

Foreign entities could perform unobtrusive cyber-reconnaissance of Internet-accessible U.S. computers and infrastructure. The technology permits an attacker to conceal points of origin by hopping through several intermediate way stations in cyberspace—including international cyberspace—making identification of an attacker a daunting challenge.

An attacker can spoof or conceal the origin of the individual hops and erase cyber-footprints from victim computers. Cyber-tools are readily available, posted to the Internet, and downloaded for anyone to use for malicious intent, regardless of the intended purpose. These tools, unlike the weapons of destruction that normally reside in the hands of military organizations, are available to anyone with the will to wreak havoc. A potential attacker can literally download a particular tool from the Internet and "point and click" to start an attack.

Thus, unlike the threats of the cold war, cyber-threats can come from almost anywhere. They can originate from any location, affect systems anywhere in the world, disguise origins and travel routes, and do it all instantaneously. The CIA focuses on threats overseas, but it is often difficult until very late in a given scenario to know whether an attack ultimately originated overseas or if an overseas computer is merely an intermediate step.

The ubiquitous nature of the cyber-threat to information systems, public or private, will come as no surprise to you. The DCI previously has emphasized the growing seriousness and significance of the emerging cyber-threat; the need to evaluate it from the perspective of both state and non-state actors; and has emphasized the intelligence community commitment to protecting our critical infrastructure.

It does not take a great deal of investment or skill on the part of an adversary to get into the cyber-attack game. As DCI Tenet pointed out, cyber-warfare is an attractive alternative to countries that may not be able to engage the U.S. militarily directly because ". . . the proliferation of personal computers has created millions of potential 'information warriors.'" Many entry-level hacking tools are readily available. "Backdoors," "Trojan horses," and "logic bombs" can be downloaded from the Internet by attackers who range in skill and vary in intent from joy riders and hackers to individuals and organizations supported by state and non-state actors.

Solar Sunrise

You may recall an October 1999 *Washington Post* report about an incident in early 1998 in which U.S. military systems were subjected to an "electronic assault," noted as "Solar Sunrise." The incident brought home to the government sector the real threat that such intrusions pose to national security. In addition, as the NIPC previously has testified, this incident galvanized agencies with foreign and domestic missions alike to coordinate their efforts.

The intruders hid their tracks by routing their attack through computer systems in the United Arab Emirates. They accessed unclassified logistics, administration, and accounting systems that control our ability to manage and deploy military forces.

The U.S. at the time could have been involved in military action in the Gulf given that tension was high because of Iraqi non-compliance with UN inspection teams. This timing raised concern in the U.S. that the intrusions were the initial stages of a cyber-attack by a hostile nation.

The U.S. response to this incident required a massive, cooperative effort by the FBI, the Justice Department's Computer Crimes Section, the Air Force office of special investigations, NASA, the defense information systems agency, the NSA, the CIA, and various computer emergency response teams from the military services and government agencies.

In the end, it was found that two young hackers in California had carried out the attacks under the direction of a hacker in Israel, himself a teenager. They gained privileged access to computers using tools available from a university Website and installed sniffer programs to collect user passwords. They created a backdoor to get back into the system and then used a patch available from another university Website to fix the vulnerability and prevent others from repeating their exploit. Unlike most hackers, they did not explore the contents of the victim computers.

The Solar Sunrise scenario points to commonality between attacks against government systems and those perpetrated against commercial systems, regardless of origin.

Emerging National Programs/Nation-States

We are detecting, with increasing frequency, the appearance of doctrine and dedicated offensive cyber-warfare programs in other countries. We have identified several, based on all-source intelligence information, that are pursuing government-sponsored offensive cyber-programs. Foreign nations have begun to include information warfare in their military doctrine, as well as their war college curricula, with respect to both defensive and offensive applications. They are developing strategies and tools to conduct information attacks. Those nations developing cyber-programs recognize the value of attacking adversary computer systems, both on the military and domestic front. Just as foreign governments and the military services have long emphasized the need to disrupt the flow of information in combat situations, they now stress the power of cyber-warfare when targeted against civilian infrastructures, particularly those that could support military strategy.

Many of the countries whose cyber-warfare programs we follow are the same ones that realize that, in a conventional military confrontation with the U.S., they will not prevail. These countries perceive that cyber-attacks, launched from within or outside the U.S., against public and private computer systems in the U.S., represent the kind of asymmetric option they will need to level the playing field during an armed crisis against the U.S.

Just as foreign governments and their military services have long emphasized—and still do—the need to disrupt the flow of information in combat situations, they now also stress the power of "information warfare" when targeted against civilian information infrastructures. The following statements by high-level foreign defense or military officials illustrate the importance of information warfare in the decades ahead.

In an interview a senior Russian official commented that an attack against a national target such as transportation or electrical power distribution would ". . . by virtue of its catastrophic consequences, completely overlap with the use of [weapons] of mass destruction."

A Chinese General indicated in a military publication in 1996 that in future wars, computers would be vulnerable in three ways. "We can make the enemy's command centers not work by changing their data system. We can cause the enemy's headquarters to make incorrect judgment by sending disinformation. We can dominate the enemy's banking system and even its entire social order."

As these anecdotes illustrate, the battle space of the information age would surely include attacks against our domestic infrastructure.

Terrorist Threat/Non-state Actors

The next group of potential adversaries comprises primarily terrorists (non-state actors) who present the most diverse and difficult threat entity to characterize. Nevertheless, we are detecting with increasing frequency the appearance and adoption of computer and Internet familiarity in the hands of these non-state actors. Some may be aligned with cults or hate groups, and still others may be sponsored by foreign industrial concerns attempting to steal proprietary information from competitors. Terrorists and other non-state actors have come to recognize that cyber-weapons offer them new, low-cost, easily hidden tools to support their causes.

The skills and resources of this threat group range from the merely troublesome to dangerous. As we now know, Middle East terrorist groups—such as Hizbollah, HAMAS, and Usama Bin Ladin's organization—are using computerized files, email, and encryption to support their organizations. We also recognize that cyber-tools offer them new, low-cost, easily hidden means to inflict damage. Terrorists and extremists already use the Internet to communicate, to raise funds, recruit, and gather intelligence. They may even launch attacks remotely from countries where their actions are not illegal or with whom we have no extradition agreements.

Terrorists, while unlikely to mount an attack on the same scale as a nation, can still do considerable harm. Moreover, the technology of hacking has advanced to the point that many tools that required in-depth knowledge a few years ago have become automated and more "user-friendly."

Cyber-attacks offer terrorists the possibility of greater security and operational flexibility. Theoretically, they can launch a computer assault from almost anywhere in the world without exposing the attacker to physical harm. Terrorists are not bound by traditional norms of political behavior between states. While a foreign state may hesitate to launch a cyber-attack against the U.S. to avoid retaliation or negative political effects, terrorists often seek the attention—and the increase in fear—which would be generated by such a cyber-attack.

Let me offer some examples: A group calling themselves the Internet Black Tigers took responsibility for attacks in August 1998 on the email systems of Sri Lankan diplomatic posts around the world, including those in the U.S. Third-country sympathizers of the Mexican Zapatista rebels crashed Webpages belonging to Mexican financial institutions. While such attacks did not result in damage to the targets, they were portrayed as successful by the activists and used to generate propaganda and rally supporters. Kurdish separatists in Greece and Turkey, Kashmiri separatists in India, and Zapatista rebels in Mexico have also hacked official government Web pages and posted anti-government propaganda and pictures.

Response Posture

Ongoing efforts under PDD-63 already have made a start toward addressing cyber-protection. The CIA and others in the intelligence community are working hard in this area to increase awareness of the threat.

There is an additional reason for focusing on the threat to our commercial sector that lies at the very heart of the problem. The foreign cyber-threat constitutes a means to harm U.S. national interests in a nontraditional way using nontraditional attacks. It is transnational in origin; transcends geographic limitations; and is wholly independent of military intervention.

Where we can make progress, we have. We have made strong and steady improvements in our all-source analytic capabilities and in intra-government coordination with respect to mutual analysis, information sharing, and computer incident responses. The intelligence community as a whole is fully engaged in developing required policy and procedures to defend against the foreign cyber-threat. The DCI last year issued instructions to intelligence agencies as an intelligence directive, "Information Operations and Intelligence Community Related Activities."

We have developed an intelligence collection strategy, further stood up analytical units, and created special training opportunities for our personnel involved in this technical discipline. The CIA has placed analytic personnel in positions where they can influence threat analysis and warning and share in the exchange of technology related to the foreign cyber-threat. We also have an active role in the exchange of information and cooperation with NIPC, the Defense Department entities—including the Joint Task Force for Computer Network Defense—and the National Security Agency. NIPC provides the very critical bridge between government and the private sector. Each of these efforts is focused on developing the capability to respond to the nation's requirement to defend against cyber-weapons that would potentially harm critical U.S. infrastructure—public or private.

This challenge will continue to grow in the years ahead—with significant national security implications. Potential adversaries have only to look to recent denial of service attacks to arrive at a full appreciation of our vulnerabilities as well as our dependencies on systems. As we all recognize, this type of cyber-threat challenges conventional intelligence methods. Intelligence disciplines traditionally have focused on physical indicators of activity and on mechanized, industrially based systems. Unless we have intelligence indications dealing with someone's intention to attack, adequate warning will be very difficult to attain.

With the advent of the cyber-threat, we are faced with the need to function in the medium of "cyberspace" where we will conduct our business in new and challenging ways.

What is missing from this testimony, and other testimony by the U.S. intelligence community, is any indication of the net threat posed to the U.S., and any net assessment of vulnerability. No mention is made of offensive response capabilities, and the focus is almost exclusively on active defense efforts. No mention is made of the need to react to the threat by designing less vulnerable or more isolated systems, improving intelligence capability to detect and attribute ongoing attacks, and using intelligence to respond/retaliate. No explicit mention is made of the need to prioritize the intelligence effort by prioritizing threats, risks, vulnerabilities, and consequences.

There are a variety of reasons for these problems. Like experts outside the intelligence community, intelligence experts in the area tend to dramatize the threat rather than analyze it. Efforts to create broad interagency intercommercial information sharing consortiums by the intelligence community have often failed due to lack of funding. Other efforts by the community to enlist private sector companies to provide technical analytic support for cyber-counterintelligence and defensive online warfare have suffered a similar fate. Such efforts may be going on, but this is not clear from either the open literature or the broad and generic nature of the cyber-defense efforts of most federal departments and agencies.

National Intelligence Council's Estimate of the Threat

At the same time, it is important to note that the National Intelligence Council has taken a broader view of the emerging threat. In its December 2000 study of global trends through the year 2015, it described the threat in terms that do far more to highlight the risk of cyber-warfare and asymmetric conflicts:[11]

> The U.S. will maintain a strong technological edge in IT-driven "battlefield awareness" and in precision-guided weaponry in 2015. The U.S. will face three types of threats:
>
> - Asymmetric threats in which state and non-state adversaries avoid direct engagements with the U.S. military but devise strategies, tactics, and weapons—some improved by "sidewise" technology—to minimize U.S. strengths and exploit perceived weaknesses;
> - Strategic WMD threats, including nuclear missile threats, in which (barring significant political or economic changes) Russia, China, most likely North Korea, probably Iran, and possibly Iraq have the capability to strike the U.S., and the potential for unconventional delivery of WMD by both states or non-state actors also will grow; and

- Regional military threats in which a few countries maintain large military forces with a mix of Cold War and post–Cold War concepts and technologies.
- Increasing reliance on computer networks is making critical U.S. infrastructures more attractive as targets. Computer network operations today offer new options for attacking the U.S. within its traditional continental sanctuary—potentially anonymously and with selective effects. Nevertheless, we do not know how quickly or effectively such adversaries as terrorists or disaffected states will develop the tradecraft to use cyber-warfare tools and technology, or, in fact, whether cyber-warfare will ever evolve into a decisive combat arm.

Asymmetric Warfare

As noted earlier, most adversaries will recognize the information advantage and military superiority of the U.S. in 2015. Rather than acquiesce to any potential U.S. military domination, they will try to circumvent or minimize U.S. strengths and exploit perceived weaknesses. IT-driven globalization will significantly increase interaction among terrorists, narcotraffickers, weapons proliferators, and organized criminals who in a networked world will have greater access to information, to technology, to finance, to sophisticated deception-and-denial techniques, and to each other. Such asymmetric approaches—whether undertaken by states or non-state actors—will become the dominant characteristic of most threats to the U.S. homeland. They will be a defining challenge for U.S. strategy, operations, and force development, and they will require that strategy to maintain focus on traditional, low-technology threats as well as the capacity of potential adversaries to harness elements of proliferating advanced technologies. At the same time, we do not know the extent to which adversaries, state and non-state, might be influenced or deterred by other geopolitical, economic, technological, or diplomatic factors in 2015.

Information Technology (IT)

Over the next 15 years, a wide range of developments will lead to many new IT-enabled devices and services. Rapid diffusion is likely because equipment costs will decrease at the same time that demand is increasing. Local-to-global Internet access holds the prospect of universal wireless connectivity via hand-held devices and large numbers of low-cost, low-altitude satellites. Satellite systems and services will develop in ways that increase performance and reduce costs.

By 2015, information technology will make major inroads in rural as well as urban areas around the globe. Moreover, information technology need not be widespread to produce important effects. The first information technology "pioneers" in each society will be the local economic and political elites, multiplying the initial impact.

- Some countries and populations, however, will fail to benefit much from the information revolution.

- Among developing countries, India will remain in the forefront in developing information technology, led by the growing class of high-tech workers and entrepreneurs.

- China will lead the developing world in utilizing information technology, with urban areas leading the countryside. Beijing's capacity to control or shape the content of information, however, is likely to be sharply reduced.

- Although most Russian urban-dwellers will adopt information technologies well before 2015, the adoption of such technologies will be slow in the broader population.

- Latin America's Internet market will grow exponentially. Argentina, Mexico, and Brazil will accrue the greatest benefits because of larger telecommunications companies, bigger markets, and more international investment.

- In Sub-Saharan Africa, South Africa is best positioned to make relatively rapid progress in IT.

Societies with advanced communications generally will worry about threats to individual privacy. Others will worry about the spread of "cultural contamination." Governments everywhere will be simultaneously asked to foster the diffusion of IT while controlling its "harmful" effects.

Discoveries in nanotechnology will lead to unprecedented understanding and control over the fundamental building blocks of all physical things. Developments in this emerging field are likely to change the way almost everything—from vaccines to computers to automobile tires to objects not yet imagined—is designed and made. Self-assembled nano-materials, such as semiconductor "quantum dots," could by 2015 revolutionize chemical labeling and enable rapid processing for drug discovery, blood content analysis, genetic analysis, and other biological applications.

Over the next 15 years, transnational criminal organizations will become increasingly adept at exploiting the global diffusion of sophisticated information, financial, and transportation networks.

Criminal organizations and networks based in North America, Western Europe, China, Colombia, Israel, Japan, Mexico, Nigeria, and Russia will expand the scale and scope of their activities. They will form loose alliances with one another, with smaller criminal entrepreneurs, and with insurgent movements for specific operations. They will corrupt leaders of unstable, economically fragile or failing states, insinuate themselves into troubled banks and businesses, and cooperate with insurgent political movements to control substantial geographic areas. Their income will come from narcotics trafficking; alien smuggling; trafficking in women and children; smuggling toxic materials, hazardous wastes, illicit arms, military technologies, and other contraband; financial fraud; and racketeering.

Available data suggest that current annual revenues from illicit criminal activities include: $100–300 billion from narcotics trafficking; $10–12 billion from toxic and other hazardous waste dumping; $9 billion from automobile theft in the U.S. and Europe; $7 billion from alien smuggling; and as much as $1 billion from theft of intellectual property through pirating of videos, software, and other commodities.

Available estimates suggest that corruption costs about $500 billion—or about 1 percent of global GNP—in slower growth, reduced foreign investment, and lower profits. For example, the average cost of bribery to firms doing business in Russia is between 4 and 8 percent of annual revenue, according to the European Bank for Reconstruction and Development.

At the same time, the trend away from state-supported political terrorism and toward more diverse, free-wheeling, transnational networks—enabled by information technology—will continue. Some of the states that actively sponsor terrorism or terrorist groups today may decrease or even cease their support by 2015 as a result of regime changes, rapprochement with neighbors, or the conclusion that terrorism has become counterproductive. But weak states also could drift toward cooperation with terrorists, creating de facto new state supporters.

Experts agree that the U.S., with its decisive edge in both information and weapons technology, will remain the dominant military power during the next 15 years. Further bolstering the strong position of the U.S. are its unparalleled economic power, its university system, and its investment in research and development—half of the total spent annually by the advanced industrial world. Many potential adversaries, as reflected in doctrinal writings and statements, see U.S. military concepts, together with technology, as giving the U.S. the ability to expand its lead in conventional warfighting capabilities.

This perception among present and potential adversaries will continue to generate the pursuit of asymmetric capabilities against U.S. forces and interests abroad as well as the territory of the U.S. U.S. opponents—state and such non-state actors as drug lords, terrorists, and foreign insurgents—will not want to engage the U.S. military on its terms. They will choose instead political and military strategies designed to dissuade the U.S. from using force, or, if the U.S. does use force, to exhaust American will, circumvent or minimize U.S. strengths, and exploit perceived U.S. weaknesses. Asymmetric challenges can arise across the spectrum of conflict that will confront U.S. forces in a theater of operations or on U.S. soil.

Threats to Critical Infrastructure

Some potential adversaries will seek ways to threaten the U.S. homeland. The U.S. national infrastructure—communications, transportation, financial transactions, energy networks—is vulnerable to disruption by physical and electronic attack because of its interdependent nature and by cyber-attacks because of their dependence on computer networks. Foreign governments and groups will seek to exploit such vulnerabilities using conventional munitions, information operations, and even WMD. Over time, such attacks increasingly are likely to be delivered by computer networks rather than by conventional munitions, as the affinity for cyber-attacks and the skill of U.S. adversaries in employing them evolve. Cyber-attacks will provide both state and non-state adversaries new options for action against the U.S. beyond mere words but short of physical attack—strategic options that include selection of either non-lethal or lethal damage and the prospect of anonymity.

Information Operations

In addition to threatening the U.S. national infrastructure, adversaries will seek to attack U.S. military capabilities through electronic warfare, psychological operations, denial and deception, and the use of new technologies such as directed energy weapons or electromagnetic pulse weapons. The primary purpose would be to deny U.S. forces information superiority, to prevent U.S. weapons from working, and to undermine U.S. domestic support for U.S. actions. Adversaries also are likely to use cyber-attacks to complicate U.S. power projection in an era of decreasing permanent U.S. military presence abroad by seeking to disrupt military networks during deployment operations—when they are most stressed. Many countries have programs to develop such technologies; few have the foresight or capability to fully integrate these various tools into a comprehensive attack. But they could develop such capabilities over the next decade and beyond.

Incidents of "Cyber-warfare": The Kosovo Crisis

Other problems in threat assessment emerge in the reporting of the Department of Defense. The department has issued a vast amount of literature on information dominance and the revolution in military affairs, but its unclassified publications barely touch upon the risk cyber-warfare poses to the U.S. and U.S. military capabilities to defend and respond. For example, Secretary of Defense William Cohen's FY2001 Annual Report to the President and Congress has a chapter titled "Information Superiority and Space," but this chapter is almost totally decoupled from any consideration of the fact that information and cyber-warfare may be used against U.S. civilians, the U.S. government as a whole, or the U.S. economy.[12] Like virtually all Department of Defense unclassified literature and testimony, the impact of cyber-warfare on the U.S. homeland is ignored. This is the mirror image of the tendency of civil departments and agencies to focus on cyber-crime, cyber-terrorism, and cracking, and ignore cyber-warfare.

As is the case with many of the emerging threats that are driving the U.S. to consider new approaches to homeland defense, it is difficult to know how far the threat can escalate or what cyber-war really means. It is clear, however, that current federal policy recognizes threats from state actors as a key factor, and there are case examples of attempts to attack that border upon cyber-warfare, and provide interesting insights into what might happen and the results for U.S. planning.

One is the course of events during the war in Kosovo. Both sides used information warfare during the Kosovo campaign. Some of this warfare involved traditional use of propaganda and the media. The U.S. stressed the importance of this aspect of information warfare in some of its reporting on the lessons of the campaign,[13]

The first political–military plan on Kosovo, completed in the fall of 1998, focused on using the threat of NATO air strikes to achieve a political-military settlement. After this threat of force convinced Milosevic to garrison most Serb forces in October 1998, interagency planning efforts focused on deploying the OSCE's Kosovo Verification Mission, facilitating humanitarian assistance, and responding to possible Serbian noncompliance. During Operation Allied Force, two interagency planning efforts occurred simultaneously. The first involved the development of a strategic campaign plan designed to ensure that wider U.S. and allied diplomatic, economic, and information efforts were integrated with our military operations.

As it became clear that Milosevic hoped to outlast the alliance, more attention was paid to other ways of bringing pressure to bear. The second effort involved planning for a NATO-led peace implementation force in Kosovo and an international civilian presence for the UN Mission in Kosovo (UNMIK) after NATO's military campaign had achieved its objectives.

This experience has taught us that our planning must better reflect the full range of instruments at our disposal, including the use of economic sanctions, public diplomacy, and other information efforts. Our initial planning focused on air strikes and diplomacy as the tools to achieve U.S. and NATO objectives. To ensure comprehensive planning and high-level awareness of the range of instruments available to decision-makers, we believe it is important that senior officials participate routinely in rehearsals, gaming, exercises, and simulations.

Successfully conducting operations to disrupt or confuse an enemy's ability to collect, process, and disseminate information is becoming increasingly important in this "information age" of warfare. The importance of such capabilities was recognized fully during Operation Allied Force, but the conduct of an integrated information operations campaign was delayed by the lack of both advance planning and strategic guidance defining key objectives. The department will address this problem by developing the needed plans and testing them in exercises.

There is good reason to "address the problem." One of the most striking aspects of any review of the propaganda campaign conducted by both sides is how inept many portions of the campaign were, how unconvincing numerous media and propaganda statements were, and how often the content lacked the depth to be convincing. In many cases, the statements also seemed to ignore the different values and perspective of the other side, and may have done more to reassure those issuing the statements than influence either the enemy or world opinion. While NATO certainly did a better job than Serbia, it failed to perform at par despite the fact that it had far more means and a far better case. It also did not avoid over-selling in shallow ways that alienated a considerable amount of the media and created a major credibility problem.

NATO was slow to attack Serbian TV and radio and deny Serbia its propaganda machine. It also followed the examples of Desert Storm and Desert Fox in giving foreign journalists a de facto sanctuary in broadcasting from enemy territory although this was done with much of the same censorship and manipulation used by Iraq in previous conflicts. There are obvious drawbacks to attacking enemy media and risking casualties among foreign journalists. There also, however, are strong advantages to taking a more aggressive stance and announcing before a conflict that foreign journalists cannot expect to be safe from attacks on enemy information centers. Serious war requires serious action.

Serbia's Role in Information Warfare

What is more relevant to critical infrastructure protection, however, is that both sides made extensive efforts to intercept the other side's communications, jam or deceive sensors, and conduct other forms of electronic warfare. In both cases, the campaign in Kosovo reinforced the critical role that information warfare can play in the broadest sense of the term.[14] One interesting aspect of the campaign was that the Internet became a new global propaganda tool for both sides, and that Serbia launched a computer attack on the NATO Web page—perhaps the first attack of its kind.

Serbia also made extensive use of another new tool in information warfare—the cellular phone. NATO experts feel that Serbians regularly observed NATO air bases and facilities, and would "phone home" to warn of NATO take-offs and probable attacks.[15] Ironically, NATO struck constantly at military relay stations but only damaged three out of about 20 telephone nodes and none of the three network control stations that supported Serbian cell phones. This left most communications and Internet access intact.[16]

Some U.S. officers, like General John Jumper, the commander of the U.S. Air Forces in Europe (USAFE) feel that the Serbs may also have been able to exploit leaks within the NATO targeting and command structure: "We were concerned about the compromise of target lists and even the air tasking order in some cases. I could not tell you if that was the result of the target process (which included non-U.S. NATO officers) or the result of leaks somewhere else in the operational and tactical system. But, yes, it was a significant concern to all of us, and in some cases I was convinced that (the Serbs) had that information (target data) ahead of time."[17]

Vice Admiral Daniel Murphy, the commander of the U.S. Sixth Fleet also noted in testimony to Congress that, "We took special care with respect to the Tomahawk and CALCM cruise missiles and our stealth technology so those missions were never made available (to NATO) in terms of precise timing or ingress and egress. We know that they weren't compromised. This was a reflection of a very real concern that senior commanders had that we didn't have airtight security within NATO."[18]

NATO's Role in Information Warfare

NATO, Serbian, and KLA units made use of the GPS system—another system open to civilian use. As a result, the distinction between civilian and military information systems was increasingly blurred—a pattern that is likely to be equally true in future conflicts.

Both also attacked the other's information and computer systems. The Serbian attacks seem to have been limited and rather crude. The most visible signs were Serbian efforts to block access to the NATO Web page on the Internet and to corrupt some of the graphics on that page. Serbia did not seem to have significant success in penetrating any major NATO communications and computer system.

NATO and the U.S. have kept most of their efforts classified, but it seems that NATO was able to penetrate some Serbian systems and either overload them with extraneous information and other "brute force" methods, or manipulate and alter data to protect some of NATO's attacking aircraft. This situation differed from the Gulf War, where the U.S. developed the ability to read Iraqi e-mail systems but did not actively attack the system. While the U.S. Air Force planned such attacks in depth, they were blocked by the U.S. intelligence community that felt that they would do more to corrupt the quality of intelligence collection than damage Iraqi operations. The CIA and National Security Agency both raised key issues about the trade-offs between information warfare and a loss of intelligence and targeting data.

The U.S. Air Force does seem to have been able to insert false targets into the Serbian air defense system—although there is no precise way to determine how much of the attempted penetration actually appeared on Serbia radars and data read outs. Although the details remain classified, the primary method of attack seems to have been the use of false radar images supported by false communications and emissions designed to deceive Serbian electronic intelligence. It seems, however, that these attacks were delayed because Kosovo had not been seen as presenting a serious risk of a large-scale air conflict, and that this delay, along with tactical failures such as repeating flight paths and a failure to defeat cell-phone-equipped civilian ground observers, contributed to the loss of one F-117 and damage to another.[19]

There are indications that the U.S. Air Force is modifying its EC-130 fleet and UAVs to allow them to intercept microwave beams and side lobes and penetrate enemy communications systems. The U.S. Army is considering adding similar capabilities to its RC-7 airborne reconnaissance systems, RC-12 Guardrails, tactical UAV, and future Airborne Common Sensor. It is also possible that the U.S. Milstar and Defense Satellite Communications System (DSCS) satellites are being modified to support computer intercept and penetration.[20]

Is Information Warfare and Retaliation Legal and Worth Its Costs?

This case study illustrates the "offensive" side of critical infrastructure protection and information warfare, and it is important to note that the problems would have been far more serious if the U.S. forces in the field had been more vulnerable, and/or the U.S. had come under serious attack by a sophisticated hostile power. U.S. information warriors must find some way to overcome the long-standing objections by the CIA and National Security Agency to direct attacks on enemy computer systems that are prime sources of intelligence. Furthermore, the Department of Defense encountered major legal objections during Kosovo to attacks using international links that might affect public and financial systems. Lawyers raised strong "law of war" arguments that information warfare can only be used against dedicated military systems, and the General Counsel's office of the Department of Defense ended up issuing some 50 pages of complex guidelines on the legal issues involved.[21]

The U.S. experience in Kosovo also raises serious questions about a potentially new form of collateral damage; the conflict between information warfare; intelligence gathering; and prohibitions on "indiscriminate attacks on civilian facilities—and how to solve the resulting organizational problems on both a national and multinational level.

Lower-Level Incidents of "Cyber-warfare"

There are a number of other incidents that illustrate the potential threat posed by cyber-warfare and high-level cyber-terrorism.

Moonlight Maze

On October 6, 1999 U.S. officials reported to Congress that extensive attacks against U.S. government systems had been underway over the period of one year. Most of the information around this incident, dubbed "Moonlight Maze" by law enforcement, remains classified. What is known, however, is that covert hackers systematically broke into the DOD's unclassified systems, the Energy Department's nuclear weapons and research labs, NASA, several agencies responsible for national infrastructure, as well as numerous academic research facilities and defense contractors' systems, siphoning off vast amounts of sensitive information.

What made these attacks alarming was the fact that the intrusions were organized, rather than random, and the volume of extracted material was unprecedented. Despite the fact that the systems that were attacked were unclassified systems they contained potentially sensitive data—including data on military logistics, planning, purchases, payrolls, personnel, and routine e-mail communications. In some instances, the perpetrators placed trapdoors on the infiltrated systems to facilitate a reentry into the system at a later date.

The attacks were traced back to an Internet service provider 20 miles outside of Moscow with strong ties to the Russian Academy of Science, which has extensive relationships with the Russian military. An analysis of the intrusions suggested that the attacks occurred during "business hours," on weekdays between 8 A.M. and 5 P.M. Russian time, but not on weekends or during Russian holidays. These facts were used to postulate that the person or persons carrying out the attacks were working in an office in Russia, possibly under the direction of local intelligence agencies or even working for organized crime groups.

The Russian Academy of Science strongly denied any involvement in the attacks, stating that anyone had access to that particular Internet service provider both domestically and internationally. Furthermore, the spokesman for the Russian foreign intelligence service stated that if Russian intelligence personnel had indeed been involved they would have not been so stupid as to engage in such activities in such a way that they could be traced straight back to Moscow. Despite intense investigations the motives and identity of the attackers were never established.

As a result of these attacks, the Pentagon decided that all its unclassified communications should pass through eight large electronic gateways rather than the thousands of connection points previously used. This would facilitate the monitoring of activities. The Pentagon also ordered $200 million in new encryption technology, upgraded intrusion detection devices, and firewalls to prevent such unauthorized use of the system in the future.

Solar Sunrise

The second case illustrating the potential risks cyber-warfare poses to the American homeland involves a case where the attacker did not turn out to be a foreign government, but the U.S. could not determine this at the time. In February and March of 1998, during heightened military tension in the Gulf due to Iraqi defiance to UN inspection teams, intruders gained access to more than 500 military, civilian, government, and private sector computer systems.[22]

According to CIA Information Operations Issue Manager John A. Serabian's Jr. in testimony before the Joint Economic Committee on Cyber-Threats to the U.S. Economy in February 2000, the intruders gained access to "unclassified logistics, administration, and accounting systems that control our ability to manage and deploy forces." The timing of the attack and the route of the attack internet service providers in the Gulf region raised the possibility that, "the intrusions were the initial stages of a cyber-attack by a hostile nation."[23] In time, it was found that the attacks were pulled off by two young hackers in California and another Israeli youth. The hackers accessed the systems "using tools available on a university Web site and installed sniffer programs to collect user passwords."[24]

In his testimony, Serabian states that this attack posed serious problems for the federal government: "The incident brought home to the government sector the real threat that such intrusions pose to national security. In addition, as NIPC previously has testified, this incident galvanized agencies with foreign and domestic missions alike to coordinate their efforts."[25]

Although the Solar Sunrise incident was not a coordinated attack by a foreign government, it was initially believed to have been one, and could have been interpreted as one. Deputy Secretary of Defense John Hamre called this the "most organized and systematic attack" on the U.S. defense systems. Even President Clinton was alerted early on that it may have been a coordinated attack by Iraq.[26]

Rome Labs Incident

On March 28, 1994 the systems administrator at Rome Air Development Center, Griffiss Air Force Base, New York—also called Rome Labs—noticed that their networks had been compromised by an illegal wire-tapping program commonly known as a "sniffer" program. Since Rome Labs is the Air Force's premier command and control research facility with projects ranging from artificial intelligence systems, radar systems, and target detection and tracking system, this intrusion was extremely troubling. Furthermore, Rome Labs is also connected to other facilities including academic institutions, commercial research facilities, and defense contractors.

An initial investigation revealed that two unknown individuals had accessed seven of Rome Labs' systems, installed sniffer programs, and gained full access to all the information residing on these systems. Using the information gleaned from the seven sniffer programs the perpetrators were able to compromise over 100 additional user accounts, read, copy, and delete user e-mail as well as read and copy sensitive unclassified battlefield simulation program data. A review of the security logs of these systems revealed that the Rome Labs' systems had initially been penetrated on March 23, 1994, five days before they were discovered.

Once all 30 of Rome Labs' systems were compromised, the attackers used Rome Labs' systems as a platform to launch attacks on other military, government, commercial, and academic systems around the world. Rather than shutting down all connections it was decided to monitor the activities of the two perpetrators to try and determine who was behind the attack and the motivation.

Investigators were able to establish that on March 30, 1994 the systems of the Army Corps of Engineers in Vicksburg, Mississippi were attacked from the Rome Labs' systems. It was also determined that the perpetrators were using the nicknames Datastream and Kuji and conferring with each other regularly. Further monitoring revealed that Kuji was by far more knowledgeable acting as a mentor and teacher to Datastream and receiving, in return, the pilfered information obtained by Datastream.

With the help of their human intelligence network, the Air Force Office of Special Investigations (AFOSI) got a tip that a hacker identifying himself as Datastream Cowboy had an e-mail exchange with the informant, stating that he was a 16-year-old from the United Kingdom who enjoyed breaking into military (.mil) sites because they were so insecure. Using this information the AFOSI agents contacted Scotland Yard who were able to identify the individuals living in the home associated with Datastream's telephone number. A monitoring of the phone numbers revealed that someone from that residence was "phone phreaking" through British Telecom. It was also discovered that originating from the UK, Datastream's path of attack was through multiple systems in multiple countries in South America, Europe, and also through Mexico and Hawaii. From Rome Labs, Datastream was able to attack systems via the Internet at NASA's Jet Propulsion Laboratory in California and their Goddard Space Flight Center in Greenbelt, Maryland.

On April 10, continuous monitoring revealed that Datastream had successfully compromised an aerospace contractor's home system enabling him to roam the system and all the system's links to it, freely. On April 12, Datastream once again used Rome Labs as a platform, this time to launch an attack against Brookhaven National Labs, Department of Energy, New York.

On April 14, monitoring of the Seattle Internet service provider, cyberspace.com, through which a number of the attacks were routed, showed that Kuji connected to Goddard Space Flight Center from Latvia and was downloading information to the Internet service provider. In order to prevent the loss of sensitive information the AFOSI agents monitoring the transfer broke the connection. Meanwhile, further monitoring of cyberspace.com revealed that Datastream accessed the National AeroSpace Plane Joint Program Office at Wright-Patterson Air Force Base in Ohio. Once again a system in Latvia was used as a hop in an attempt to avoid identification.

On April 15, Kuji attempted to break into NATO Headquarters in Brussels. Though unsuccessful in this particular attack, a subsequent interview with the system administrator from SHAPE Technical Center (NATO Headquarters) brought to light that Datastream had successfully penetrated SHAPE's computer systems in a previous instance.

Having confirmed the identity of the hacker and established probable cause, Scotland Yard was able to obtain a search warrant. It was decided that the warrant should be executed while the hacker was online so as to allow the investigators to establish the identity of all the victims in the path between Datastream's computer and Rome Labs' systems. As they waited the monitoring team realized that Datastream had suddenly accessed a Korean Atomic Research Institute and was downloading all the information from that facility onto Rome Labs' systems. Frantic scrambling ensued since the investigators were not sure whether it was a North or South Korean facility that was being targeted. The concern was that if it was a North Korean facility then the intrusion could be construed as an act of war by the United States since it would look to the Korean's as if the intrusion and transfer of data were carried out by the U.S. Air Force. This was especially troubling since the U.S. was in the midst of sensitive negotiations with the North Koreans regarding their nuclear weapons program precisely at this time. As it turned out the attack luckily targeted a South Korean nuclear research facility and major political embarrassment or worse was avoided. At this point British authorities decided to delay the execution of the search warrant and to expand their monitoring activities with the help of the Air Force investigators.

On May 12, the search warrant was finally served and it was discovered that Datastream was a 16-year-old youth using a 25MHz 486 SX desktop computer with only 170 megabytes (which is a very modest computer) to carry out the attacks. Datastream admitted to breaking into Rome Labs on numerous occasions as well as compromising a number of other military and government systems. He also admitted to searching the systems for information relating to missiles with a specific interest in artificial intelligence. He also disclosed that, in one instance, he stole a 3–4 megabyte file on artificial intelligence program that dealt with the Air Order of Battle which he stored on the Internet service provider's systems since his computer did not have enough storage space. To pay for the Internet service provider, Datastream explained that he used a fraudulent credit card number that was generated using a hacker tool he found on the Internet.

After extensive interviewing, Datastream was released on bail. Despite intense investigations the identity and motives of the Kuji were never discovered and unfortunately Datastream provided a lot of the stolen information to Kuji. What was done with the information provided to Kuji and stolen by him in the 26-day attack and whom it was intended for is still a mystery.[27]

On October 31, 1994 a damage assessment was conducted of the intrusion into the Rome Labs. It was estimated that the total loss incurred by the U.S. Air Force was $211,722 but this did not include the investigative costs or that of the monitoring and recovery team. Also, no other federal agency that was a victim of these attacks did a damage assessment.[28]

THE COMPUTER SECURITY INSTITUTE'S SURVEY OF THE THREAT

There are only limited nongovernmental data on the threats to critical infrastructure, and some aspects of these estimates—particularly the cost data—are suspect. Like most official data, such statistics are also concerned largely with the sheer volume of hacking/cracking, cyber-crime, and low-level cyber-terrorism. The data that is available, however, clearly confirms the fact that the growth in dependence on information systems has led to a steady growth in the number of attacks and incidents. Although, the U.S. has not yet experienced more than a limited number of terrorist attacks and has not been the subject of a coherent attack by any state actor.

The Computer Security Institute or CSI, was established in 1974 and is a San Francisco-based association of information security professionals. It has thousands of members worldwide and provides a wide variety of information and education programs to assist practitioners in protecting the information assets of corporations and governmental organizations. It released its fifth annual "Computer Crime and Security Survey" in March 2000. This survey was conducted with the participation of the San Francisco FBI Computer Intrusion Squad and highlighted statistics citing estimated financial losses and the number of times government and corporation systems have been compromised in some fashion. The survey was based on the responses of 643 computer security practitioners in U.S. corporations, government agencies, financial institutions, medical institutions, and universities.

According to CSI, the survey "confirms that the threat from computer crime and other information security breaches continues unabated and that the financial toll is mounting." The survey reported that 273 organizations that could quantify their losses were forced to deal with $265.6 million in financial losses due to cyber-attacks. These estimates were up from $123.7 million reported by 163 organizations in 1999. The survey listed the loss of proprietary information (accounting for $66,708,000 in losses) and financial fraud (accounting for $55,996,000 in losses).[29]

The CSI reported the following detailed results[30]

- Ninety percent of survey respondents detect cyber-attacks, 273 organizations report $265,589,940 in financial losses.

- Ninety percent of respondents (primarily large corporations and government agencies) detected computer security breaches within the last twelve months.

- Seventy percent reported a variety of serious computer security breaches other than the most common ones of computer viruses, laptop theft or employee "net abuse"—for example, theft of proprietary information, financial fraud, system penetration from outsiders, denial of service attacks, and sabotage of data or networks.

- Seventy-four percent acknowledged financial losses due to computer breaches.
- Forty-two percent were willing and/or able to quantify their financial losses. The losses from these 273 respondents totaled $265,589,940 (the average annual total over the last three years was $120,240,180).
- Financial losses in eight of twelve categories were larger than in any previous year. Furthermore, financial losses in four categories were higher than the combined total of the three previous years. For example, 61 respondents quantified losses due to sabotage of data or networks for a total of $27,148,000. The total financial losses due to sabotage for the previous years combined totaled only $10,848,850.
- As in previous years, the most serious financial losses occurred through theft of proprietary information (66 respondents reported $66,708,000) and financial fraud (53 respondents reported $55,996,000).
- Survey results illustrate that computer crime threats to large corporations and government agencies come from both inside and outside their electronic perimeters, confirming the trend in previous years. Seventy-one percent of respondents detected unauthorized access by insiders. But for the third year in a row more respondents (59%) cited their Internet connection as a frequent point of attack than cited their internal systems as a frequent point of attack (38%).
- Based on responses from 643 computer security practitioners in U.S. corporations, government agencies, financial institutions, medical institutions, and universities the findings of the "2000 Computer Crime and Security Survey" confirm that the threat from computer crime and other information security breaches continues unabated and that the financial toll is mounting.
- Respondents detected a wide range of attacks and abuses:
  - 25% of respondents detected system penetration from the outside.
  - 27% of respondents detected denial of service attacks.
  - 79% detected employee abuse of Internet access privileges (for example, downloading pornography or pirated software, or inappropriate use of e-mail systems).
  - 85% detected computer viruses.
- Most of the respondents conducted electronic commerce over the Internet. Here are some of the results:
  - 93% of respondents have Web sites.
  - 43% conduct electronic commerce on their sites (in 1999 it was only 30%).
  - 19% suffered unauthorized access or misuse within the last twelve months.

- 32% said that they didn't know if there had been unauthorized access or misuse.
- 35% of those acknowledging attacks reported from two to five incidents.
- 19% reported ten or more incidents.
- 64% of those acknowledging an attack reported Web site vandalism.
- 60% reported denial of service.
- 8% reported theft of transaction information.
- 3% reported financial fraud.

Patrice Rapalus, Director of the CSI, commented that,[31]

The trends the CSI/FBI survey has highlighted over the years are disturbing. Cyber-crimes and other information security breaches are widespread and diverse. Ninety percent of respondents reported attacks. Furthermore, such incidents can result in serious damages. The 273 organizations that were able to quantify their losses reported a total of $265,589,940. Clearly, more must be done in terms of adherence to sound practices, deployment of sophisticated technologies, and most importantly adequate staffing and training of information security practitioners in both the private sector and government.

Bruce J. Gebhardt, agent in charge of the FBI's Northern California office, has responsibility for a division covering fifteen counties, including the Silicon Valley area, and commented that,

If the FBI and other law enforcement agencies are to be successful in combating this continually increasing problem, we cannot always be placed in a reactive mode, responding to computer crises as they happen. The results of the CSI/FBI survey provide us with valuable data. This information not only has been shared with Congress to underscore the need for additional investigative resources on a national level but identifies emerging crime trends and helps me decide how best to proactively and aggressively assign resources before those "trends" become "crises."

It should be noted, however, that such statistics are difficult to put in perspective, and have all of the problems in terms of their lack of statistical consistency, cost methodology, and lack of prioritization cited earlier. It is difficult to determine the importance of any given information system and to measure how serious any given attack will be. Almost all users see *their* system as critical. From the outside, however, many systems seem to have only marginal value, while others can be degraded or interrupted with only limited damage.

COMPUTER EMERGENCY RESPONSE TEAM'S (CERT) ASSESSMENT OF THREAT

The CERT Coordination Center, located at the Software Engineering Institute (SEI) at Carnegie Mellon University was created in 1988 in the aftermath of an Internet worm incident that halted 10 percent of Internet systems at the time. The Center was funded by the Defense Advanced Research Projects Agency (DARPA) in order to create a "center to co-ordinate communication among experts during security emergencies and to help prevent future incidents."[32] Since its inception, CERT has handled over "28,000 computer network security incidents and analyzed more that 1,500 vulnerabilities in network related products."[33]

CERT assessments of the current state of information security focus on the increased vulnerability of the Internet. In testimony before the Senate Judiciary Committee on May 25, 2000, CERT Director Richard D. Pethia stated that "vulnerabilities associated with the Internet put government, business, and individual users at risk. Security measures that were appropriate for mainframe computers and small well-defined networks inside an organization are not effective for the Internet. . . ."[34] Traditional rules do not apply within this Internet world because of the lack of well-defined boundaries.

Pethia also points to the increasingly sophisticated yet more user-friendly intruder tools that are widely available as a large vulnerability of the Internet. Pethia predicts that with new "distributed-system attack tools" intruders will be able to launch attacks which can strike large numbers of sites simultaneously, in turn focusing all of these sites to attack one or several systems, hosts or networks.[35]

Pethia lists several factors that shape the balance the vulnerability of Internet security.[36]

- Because of the dramatically lower cost of communication on the Internet, use of the Internet is replacing other forms of electronic communication. The Internet itself is growing at an amazing rate as noted in an earlier section.

- There is a continuing movement to distributed, client-server, and heterogeneous configurations. As the technology is being distributed, so is the management of that technology. In these cases, system administration and management often fall upon people who do not have the training, skill, resources, or interest needed to operate their systems securely. The number of directly connected homes, schools, libraries and other venues without trained system administration and security staff is rapidly increasing. These "always-on, rarely protected" systems allow attackers to continue to add new systems to their arsenal of captured weapons.

- Internet sites have become so interconnected and intruder tools so effective that the security of any site depends, in part, on the security of all other sites on the Internet.

- The difficulty of criminal investigation of cyber-crime coupled with the complexity of international law mean that successful apprehension and prosecution of computer criminals is unlikely, and thus little deterrent value is realized.

- The Internet is becoming increasingly complex and dynamic, but among those connected to the Internet there is a lack of adequate knowledge about the network and about security. The rush to the Internet, coupled with a lack of understanding, is leading to the exposure of sensitive data and risk to safety-critical systems. Misconfigured or outdated operating systems, mail programs, and Web sites result in vulnerabilities that intruders can exploit. Just one naïve user with an easy-to-guess password increases an organization's risk.

- When vendors release patches or upgrades to solve security problems, organizations' systems often are not upgraded. The job may be too time-consuming, too complex, or just at too low a priority for the system administration staff to handle. With increased complexity comes the introduction of more vulnerabilities, so solutions do not solve problems for the long term—system maintenance is never-ending. Because managers do not fully understand the risks, they neither give security a high enough priority nor assign adequate resources. Exacerbating the problem is the fact that the demand for skilled system administrators far exceeds the supply.

- As we face the complex and rapidly changing world of the Internet, comprehensive solutions are lacking. Among security-conscious organizations, there is increased reliance on "silver bullet" solutions, such as firewalls and encryption. The organizations that have applied a "silver bullet" are lulled into a false sense of security and become less vigilant, but single solutions applied once are neither foolproof nor adequate. Solutions must be combined, and the security situation must be constantly monitored as technology changes and new exploitation techniques are discovered.

- There is little evidence of improvement in the security features of most products; developers are not devoting sufficient effort to apply lessons learned about the sources of vulnerabilities. The CERT Coordination Center routinely receives reports of new vulnerabilities. We continue to see the same types of vulnerabilities in newer versions of products that we saw in earlier versions. Technology evolves so rapidly that vendors concentrate on time to market, often minimizing that time by placing a low priority on security features. Until their customers demand products that are more secure, the situation is unlikely to change.

- Engineering for ease of use is not being matched by engineering for ease of secure administration. Today's software products, workstations, and personal computers bring the power of the computer to increasing numbers of people who use that power to perform their work more efficiently. Products are so easy to use that people with little technical knowledge or skill can install and operate them on their desktop computers. Unfortunately, it is difficult to configure and operate many of these products securely. This gap leads to increasing numbers of vulnerable systems.

Once again, it is obvious that basic questions need to be asked about the importance of the attacks being counted. The tacit assumption seems to be that government and the private sector are slow to react and often negligent. This may be the case, but it is also possible that many of the problems Pethia cites occur because the attacks to date have simply not been that important and/or are only part of a broad pattern of problems with crime, systems failures, and unrelated problems that have higher priority.

At the same time, Pethia is one of the few experts to stress that cyber-system design, and reducing information system vulnerability, is as important as active defense. Unfortunately, far too much of the public literature seems to be written from the perspective of those involved in active commercial cyber-defense, rather than from the broader perspective of finding solutions that meet the needs of homeland defense In order to respond to the overall priorities of government and the private sector, and examine the cost-effectiveness of the full range of possible solutions, a shift in perspective will be required.

CHALLENGES IN IMPROVING THE ASSESSMENT OF THE THREAT

These threat assessments show that the federal government and the private sector recognize the broad nature of the threat and its complexity. They also show that the threat is evolving rapidly and may change sharply in the future in both character and intensity. As a result, it is difficult to argue for more precision in characterizing the threat, or that the federal government should adopt some standard definition of the threat. In practice, the government is likely to be far better off if it reacts to the evolution of events, rather than to be bound by over-defined terms that quickly become out of date.

At the same time, a survey of current federal reports and other threat assessments does reveal the need to make every effort to improve the current methodology for assessing the threat. It also reveals several major problems that clearly need to be addressed such as improving intelligence, and improving both government and civil programs to deal with these threats:

- It is far easier to know that a system is under attack than to measure the cost of the attack in dollars, human lives, or social impact. This is sometimes disguised by issuing cost estimates, but in virtually every case such estimates are little more than speculation, and often uninformed speculation at that. The problem is exacerbated by the fact that some organizations set different thresholds for attack, such as counting reconnaissance or errant packets as attacks. The cyber-community is undoubtedly of vital importance to the U.S., but it as yet has limited credibility in quantifying and prioritizing its own importance.

- There is a lack of technological net assessment of the rapidly evolving race between cyber-offense and cyber-defense that compounds the problem. Countless assertions are being made about the threat, defense, and offense that either are not tied to or lack any detailed assessment of current capability and probable trends. The lack of such explicit net assessments is a major failing in the vulnerability analyses and the program and budget justifications of virtually every federal program dealing with critical infrastructure protection. As will be discussed later, this endemic failure is then compounded by the lack of other basic management information: A clear plan, cost, and schedule for deploying new technologies and capabilities; a detailed threat assessment to justify the specific activity involved, and an assessment of the projected technological vulnerability and cost to defeat the activity.

- While the national security community does concentrate on the correlation between critical infrastructure protection and terrorism and war, civil agencies sometimes do not seem to consider high levels of attack in any detail, and consider only those forms of "terrorism" which approximate the levels of damage they cope with in dealing with other causes of incidents. As a result, there is a clear need to establish the different levels of attack for which each federal agency must plan, and provide better and more standardized threat assessments and scenarios which ensure that federal, state, local, and civil planners fully understand the kind of contingencies they must plan for.

- There are major challenges for cyber-intelligence which go beyond trying to cope with the rapid changes in technology—a daunting challenge in itself. One is deciding how much of the burden of detecting and characterizing attacks must go to the intelligence community versus the federal, state, local, or civil entities. Another is determining the nature and scale of the attack in near real time. There are major problems in identifying attackers and the routes they use, and domestic attackers may well use foreign servers or proxies. These data must be accurate enough to target attackers if the U.S. is to retaliate and counterattack. If complex, multiple attacks occur, the intelligence community needs some basis for triage based on both vulnerability and importance. All of these factors call for both new skills and that the resources assigned to cyber-intelligence and threat assessment grow in proportion to American dependence on information systems—something that so far has not begun to take place.

- As is the case with CBRN terrorism, the laws and regulations affecting threat assessment need to be reviewed to ensure that there is a smooth and immediate flow of critical data from civil law enforcement agencies to the intelligence community and vice versa. The same holds true for the information flow from government and civil users to the intelligence community and vice versa. This can present major challenges in terms of the constraints now imposed by civil law and human rights considerations.

Chapter 3

Evolving U.S. Policy and Response

Given these problems, it is not surprising that the U.S. government is finding it difficult to determine the right way to defend America's rapidly changing critical infrastructure. There is, as yet, no clear definition of the boundaries between the kinds of attack where the federal government should play a role and those where states, localities, the private sector, and private individuals must assume responsibility for their own defense. There are countless gray areas where the federal government is implying it has some responsibility, but it may be incapable of effective action and practical responsibility—and criminal and civil liability for the failure to create effective defenses—may have to be assumed by state and local officials, the private sector, and private individuals.

Many of the changes in U.S. policy toward critical infrastructure protection have been driven largely by the increasing dependence of government and the civil sector on computers and communications networks. At the same time, the federal government has had to acknowledge and accept the fact that it is the civil sector that leads in most aspects of information technology. With the exception of electronic and communications intelligence, the private sector has outpaced government in terms of research and development and the use of advanced information systems.[37]

THE BEGINNINGS: THE COMPUTER SECURITY ACT AND CLINGER-COHEN ACT

To its credit, however, the federal government has recognized many of these problems and has already made major changes in its critical infrastructure protection and information warfare policy and efforts. The U.S. began to treat information warfare as a major new threat in the mid-1980s and began to consider the emerging threat of cyber-attacks and cyber-crime. Since that time it has created a wide range of programs which are already funded at over $2 billion a year, many of which involve partnerships with state and local governments and the private and civil sector.

The first major legislation relating to information security was passed in 1987 in the form of the Computer Security Act. This bill was enacted to "provide for a computer standards program within the National Bureau of Standards (now NIST) to provide for government-wide computer security, and to provide for the training in security matters of persons who are involved in the management operation and use of federal computer systems, and for other purposes."[38] The act required the National Bureau of Standards to:

- Establish computer standards and guidelines for federal computer systems.
- Draw upon computer system technical security guidelines developed by the National Security Agency.

The Computer Security Act also established a computer system security and Privacy Advisory Board within the Department of Commerce and among other things requires each agency to provide mandatory periodic training in computer security for all employees who manage, use, or operate computer systems. The act also stipulates that each federal agency with computer systems establish a plan for the security and privacy of sensitive information, the plans to which go to the Bureau of Standards and NSA for advice and comment.

In many cases, however, the act did not lead to effective action either within given departments and agencies or on any coordinated basis. Coordination with state and local governments was limited and little effort was made to create an effective partnership with the private and civil sectors. The Computer Security Act remained the major piece of federal computer security legislation until the mid-1990s, and budget, resources, and technical expertise remained very limited.

This situation began to change in the mid-1990s as increased dependence on information systems drew growing attention to computer and information systems security. The Office of Information and Regulatory Affairs was created under the Paperwork Reduction Act of 1995 and was given the responsibility of developing and overseeing the implementation of policies, principles, standards, and guidelines on privacy confidentiality, security, disclosure, and sharing of information collected or maintained by or for agencies. It was also tasked with making sure that they were in compliance with sections of the Computer Security Act of 1987 and required that federal agencies identify and afford security protections commensurate with the risk and magnitude of the harm resulting from the loss, misuse, or unauthorized access to or modification of information collected or maintained by or on behalf of an agency.[39]

Under the same act, federal agencies were given the responsibility with respect to information privacy and security of implementing and enforcing "applicable policies, procedures, standards, and guidelines on privacy, confidentiality, security, disclosure, and sharing of information collected or maintained by or for the agency" and remain consistent with the Computer Security Act.

In 1996 the Clinger-Cohen Act created the position of Chief Information Officer (CIO) within government agencies to ensure information systems are acquired and managed properly. The act also called for the Secretary of Commerce, based upon the standards developed by NIST, to "promulgate standards and guidelines pertaining to federal computer systems" to which "the secretary shall make such standards compulsory and binding to the extent to which the secretary determines necessary to improve the efficiency of operation or security and privacy of federal computer systems."[40] In addition, the act made OMB the agency responsible for the overall management of information technology procurement, investment, and security.

The Clinger-Cohen Act defined the protection of information systems as "with respect to an executive agency means any equipment or interconnected system or subsystem of equipment that is used in the automatic acquisition, storage, manipulation, management, movement, control, display, switching, interchange, transmission, or reception of data or information by the executive agency." The act did not, however, establish a clear tie between protecting information systems and critical infrastructure protection.

THE FEDERAL GOVERNMENT REDEFINES CRITICAL INFRASTRUCTURE AND AGENCY RESPONSIBILITIES

Since that time, there have been four major cyber-security/critical infrastructure initiatives that shape the way in which the government is responding to the new threats to information systems which help explain the current course, organization, and funding of federal programs:

- President Clinton's Executive Order 13010 of July 15, 1996, establishing the President's Commission on Critical Infrastructure Protection (PCCIP). The commission's task was to review and recommend a national policy for protecting critical infrastructures.
- The Report of the President's Commission on Critical Infrastructure Protection (PCCIP) Commission report of October 1997.
- Presidential Decision Directive 63 of May 1998. PDD-63 calls outline the base federal policy for protecting cyber-systems from threats to the critical infrastructures.
- The National Plan for Information Systems Protection, Version 1.0. released in January 7, 2000.

Executive Order 13010

The Clinton Administration issued Executive Order 13010 on July 15, 1996. This order recognized that[41]

Certain national infrastructures are so vital that their incapacity or destruction would have a debilitating impact on the defense or economic security of the United States. These critical infrastructures include telecommunications, electrical power systems, gas and oil storage and transportation, banking and finance, transportation, water supply systems, emergency services (including medical, police, fire, and rescue), and continuity of government. Threats to these critical infrastructures fall into two categories: physical threats to tangible property ("physical threats") and threats of electronic, radio frequency, or computer-based attacks on the information or communications components that control critical infrastructures ("cyber-threats"). Because many of these critical infrastructures are owned and operated by the private sector, it is essential that the government and private sector work together to develop a strategy for protecting them and assuring their continued operation.

The administration defined critical infrastructures as including "telecommunications, electrical power systems, gas and oil storage and transportation, banking and finance, transportation, water supply systems, emergency services (including medical, police, fire and rescue), and the continuity of government." A further distinction was made in dividing critical infrastructures threats categorically into physical and electronic or computer based threats.

Executive Order 13010 established the President's Commission on Critical Infrastructure Protection (PCCIP) to be chaired by an individual from outside the government and made up of individuals nominated by cabinet officials from both government and private sector. The members included head of each of the following executive branch departments and agencies: Department of the Treasury; Department of Justice; Department of Defense; Department of Commerce; Department of Transportation; Department of Energy; Central Intelligence Agency; Federal Emergency Management Agency; Federal Bureau of Investigation; and the National Security Agency.

The commission had a cabinet-level principles committee, a steering committee with four members appointed by the President, and an advisory composed of ten individuals appointed by the President from the private sector who were knowledgeable about critical infrastructures. The advisory committee was to advise the commission on the subjects of the commission's mission in whatever manner the advisory committee, the commission chair, and the steering committee deemed appropriate.

The Executive Order also established an Infrastructure Protection Task Force ("IPTF") within the Department of Justice, chaired by the Federal Bureau of Investigation. The IPTF was to undertake an interim coordinating mission with at least one full-time member each from the Federal Bureau of Investigation, the Department of Defense, and the National Security Agency as well as to identify and coordinate existing expertise, inside and outside of the federal government, to:

- Provide, or facilitate and coordinate the provision of, expert guidance on critical infrastructures, to detect, prevent, halt, or confine an attack, and to recover and restore service;
- Issue threat and warning notices in the event advance information is available about a threat;
- Provide training and education on methods of reducing vulnerabilities and responding to attacks on critical infrastructures;
- Conduct after-action analysis to determine possible future threats, targets, or methods of attack; and
- Coordinate with the pertinent law enforcement authorities during or after an attack to facilitate any resulting criminal investigation.

The President's Commission on Critical Infrastructure Protection

The President's Commission on Critical Infrastructure Protection reported in October 1997. The commission's report categorized the threats to the national infrastructure threats as being both physical and cyber, but focused on cyber-threats because they were "new and not well understood." The report found that:

- The U.S. growing dependence on information systems to run critical infrastructures leaves the country more vulnerable to both physical and, more importantly, cyber-threats
- The rapid spread of the computer related technology has given more people the tools to cheaply and effectively strike at critical infrastructures
- Threats to critical infrastructures come from a wide variety of sources
- There is a lack of awareness concerning the vulnerabilities faced
- There is no national focus or advocate for infrastructure protection
- Infrastructure assurance is a "shared responsibility" and calls for the adoption of infrastructure protection best practices, increased research and development, and the adoption of a national organization structure.[42]

The report offered several base recommendations for actions the government should take to protect infrastructure. The commission found that the growing role information systems played in the running of critical infrastructures leaves the U.S. with a growing list of vulnerabilities and threats. Added to this, the commission found this dependence could be more easily exploited with the growth and spread of computer technology.

Most importantly, the commission found that there is "a lack of awareness" on the part of both the public and government officials. The commission also drew attention to what they saw as a problem of "no national focus" on the part of the government. For the latter charge, the commission did not advocate a consolidation of infrastructure protection in the hands of one federal agency. For the commission "infrastructures are so varied, and form such a large part of this nation's economic activity, that no one person or organization can be in charge. We do not need and probably cannot stand, the appointment of a director of infrastructures. We do need, and recommend, several more modest ways to create and maintain a national focus on the issues."[43]

From these findings, the commission concluded that the government should adapt its thinking to the new rules of cyberspace, act now to protect from future threats, and come to the realization that infrastructure protection is a "shared responsibility" in which government and private industry share the burden for infrastructure protection.

The commission recommended a series of actions the government should take. First, the commission suggested a "broad program of awareness and education" in which the federal government would convene conferences and presentations and develop curricula to inform industry leaders, government officials, and the general public of the growing importance of cyber-security. Second, the commission recommended that the government promote "infrastructure protection through industry cooperation and information sharing." Third, the review of laws concerning infrastructure protection was recommended in order for the law to catch up with the pace of technology. Finally, the commission called for a revised program of research and development and a national organization structure for infrastructure protection.[44]

Presidential Decision Directive-63 (PDD-63)

Largely as a result of the PCCIP's recommendations on critical infrastructure protection, the Clinton Administration set forth a national "Policy on Critical Infrastructure Protection," also known as Presidential Decision Directive-63 (PDD-63) on May 22, 1998. PDD-63 defined critical infrastructures as "those physical and cyber-based systems essential to the minimum operations of the economy and government. They include, but are not limited to, telecommunications, energy, banking and finance, transportation, water systems and emergency services, both governmental and private." It recognized that increased automation of infrastructure is so dependent on information systems that critical infrastructure protection must be tied to information warfare.

The white paper the White House issued along with PDD-63 gave the following rationale for the new PDD:[45]

The U.S. possesses both the world's strongest military and its largest national economy. Those two aspects of our power are mutually reinforcing and dependent. They are also increasingly reliant upon certain critical infrastructures and upon cyber-based information systems.

Critical infrastructures are those physical and cyber-based systems essential to the minimum operations of the economy and government. They include, but are not limited to, telecommunications, energy, banking and finance, transportation, water systems and emergency services, both governmental and private. Many of the nation's critical infrastructures have historically been physically and logically separate systems that had little interdependence. As a result of advances in information technology and the necessity of improved efficiency, however, these infrastructures have become increasingly automated and interlinked. These same advances have created new vulnerabilities to equipment failures, human error, weather and other natural causes, and physical and cyber-attacks. Addressing these vulnerabilities will necessarily require flexible, evolutionary approaches that span both the public and private sectors, and protect both domestic and international security.

Because of our military strength, future enemies, whether nations, groups or individuals, may seek to harm us in non-traditional ways including attacks within the U.S. Our economy is increasingly reliant upon interdependent and cyber-supported infrastructures and non-traditional attacks on our infrastructure and information systems may be capable of significantly harming both our military power and our economy.

The directive acknowledged the growing threats to the U.S.' critical infrastructure, especially its cyber-systems and outlined general goals for the government response to these threats:[46]

No later than the year 2000, the U.S. shall have achieved an initial operating capability and not later than five years from the day the president signed Presidential Decision Directive 63 the U.S. shall have achieved and shall maintain the ability to protect our nation's critical infrastructures from intentional acts that would significantly diminish the abilities of the federal government to perform essential national security missions and to ensure the general public health and safety; state and local governments to maintain order and to deliver minimum essential public services; the private sector to ensure the orderly functioning of the economy and the delivery of essential telecommunications, energy, financial and transportation services.

Any interruptions or manipulations of these critical functions must be brief, infrequent, manageable, geographically isolated and minimally detrimental to the welfare of the U.S.

New Federal Guidelines

The directive laid out the guidelines for the federal effort to address potential vulnerabilities.

We shall consult with, and seek input from, Congress on approaches and programs to meet the objectives set forth in this directive.

The protection of our critical infrastructures is necessarily a shared responsibility and partnership between owners, operators, and the government. Furthermore, the federal government shall encourage international cooperation to help manage this increasingly global problem.

Frequent assessments shall be made of our critical infrastructures' existing reliability, vulnerability, and threat environment because, as technology and the nature of the threats to our critical infrastructures will continue to change rapidly, so must our protective measures and responses be robustly adaptive.

The incentives that the market provides are the first choice for addressing the problem of critical infrastructure protection; regulation will be used only in the face of a material failure of the market to protect the health, safety, or well being of the American people. In such cases, agencies shall identify and assess available alternatives to direct regulation, including providing economic incentives to encourage the desired behavior, or providing information upon which choices can be made by the private sector. These incentives, along with other actions, shall be designed to help harness the latest technologies, bring about global solutions to international problems, and enable private sector owners and operators to achieve and maintain the maximum feasible security.

The full authorities, capabilities, and resources of the government, including law enforcement, regulation, foreign intelligence, and defense preparedness shall be available, as appropriate, to ensure that critical infrastructure protection is achieved and maintained.

Care must be taken to respect privacy rights. Consumers and operators must have confidence that information will be handled accurately, confidentially, and reliably.

The federal government shall, through its research, development, and procurement, encourage the introduction of increasingly capable methods of infrastructure protection.

The federal government shall serve as a model to the private sector on how infrastructure assurance is best achieved and shall, to the extent feasible, distribute the results of its endeavors.

We must focus on preventative measures as well as threat and crisis management. To that end, private sector owners and operators should be encouraged to provide maximum feasible security for the infrastructures they control and to provide the government necessary information to assist them in that task. In order to engage the private sector fully, it is preferred that participation by owners and operators in a national infrastructure protection system be voluntary.

Close cooperation and coordination with state and local governments and first responders is essential for a robust and flexible infrastructure protection program. All critical infrastructure protection plans and actions shall take into consideration the needs, activities and responsibilities of state and local governments and first responders.

Lead Agencies for Sector Liaison

PDD-63 also established a new federal organization for critical infrastructure protection with four major elements. The first was to create lead agencies for sector liaison: For each infrastructure sector that could be a target for significant cyber or physical attacks, a single U.S. government department was designated to serve as the lead agency for liaison. Each lead agency designated one individual of assistant secretary rank or higher to be the sector liaison official for that area and to cooperate with the private sector representatives (sector coordinators) in addressing problems related to critical infrastructure protection and, in particular, to recommend components of a National Infrastructure Assurance Plan. Together, the lead agency and the private sector counterparts were to develop and implement a vulnerability awareness and education program for their sector.

- Commerce: Information and communications
- Treasury: Banking and finance
- EPA: Water supply
- Transportation: Aviation; Highways (including trucking and intelligent transportation systems); Mass Transit; Pipelines; Rail; Waterborne commerce
- Justice/FBI; Emergency law enforcement services
- FEMA: Emergency fire service and continuity of government services
- HHS: Public health services, including prevention, surveillance, laboratory services, and personal health services
- Energy: Electric power, oil, and gas production and storage

Lead Agencies for Special Functions

The second element was to establish lead agencies for special functions. These were functions related to critical infrastructure protection that must be chiefly performed by the federal government (national defense, foreign affairs, intelligence, and law enforcement). For each of those special functions, a lead agency was made responsible for coordinating all of the activities of the U.S. government in that area. Each lead agency appointed a senior officer of assistant secretary rank or higher to serve as the functional coordinator for that function for the federal government.

The lead agencies for special functions were:

- Justice/FBI: Law enforcement and internal security
- CIA: Foreign intelligence
- State: Foreign affairs
- Defense: National defense

In addition, the Office of Science and Technology Policy (OSTP) was made responsible for coordinating research and development agendas and programs for the government through the National Science and Technology Council. Furthermore, while Commerce is the lead agency for information and communication, the Department of Defense will retain its Executive Agent responsibilities for the National Communications System and support of the President's National Security Telecommunications Advisory Committee.

A New Structure for Interagency Coordination

The third element was to create a formal structure for interagency coordination: The sector liaison officials and functional coordinators of the lead agencies, as well as representatives from other relevant departments and agencies, including the National Economic Council, were tasked with coordinating the implementation of this directive under the auspices of a Critical Infrastructure Coordination Group (CICG). This effort was chaired by the National Coordinator for Security, Infrastructure Protection and Counter-Terrorism.

The National Coordinator was to be appointed by and report to the President through the Assistant to the President for National Security Affairs, who should ensure appropriate coordination with the Assistant to the President for Economic Affairs. Agency representatives to the CICG should be at a senior policy level (assistant secretary or higher). The CICG was to be assisted by extant policy structures, such as the Security Policy Board, Security Policy Forum and the National Security and Telecommunications and Information System Security Committee.

The National Coordinator was to report to the President through the Assistant to the President for National Security Affairs. The National Coordinator was also to participate as a full member in principal committee meetings when they meet to consider infrastructure issues. Although the National Coordinator is not supposed to direct departments and agencies, he or she was tasked with ensuring interagency coordination for policy development and implementation and reviewing crisis activities concerning infrastructure events with significant foreign involvement. The National Coordinator was to provide advice, in the context of the established annual budget process, regarding agency budgets for critical infrastructure protection. The National Coordinator was to chair the critical infrastructure coordination group (CICG), reporting to the deputies committee (or, at the call of its chair, the principals committee). The sector liaison officials and special function coordinators who attended the CIGC meetings and departments and agencies were each to appoint to the CIGC a senior official (assistant secretary level or higher) to regularly attend its meetings. The National Security Advisor was to appoint a senior director for infrastructure protection on the NSC staff.

A National Plan Coordination (NPC) staff was to be contributed on a non-reimbursable basis by the departments and agencies, consistent with law. The NPC staff was tasked to integrate the various sector plans into a National Infrastructure Assurance Plan and coordinate analyses of the U.S. government's own dependencies on critical infrastructures.

The NPC staff was also tasked to help coordinate a national education and awareness program, and legislative and public affairs. The Defense Department was to continue to serve as Executive Agent for the Commission Transition Office, which would form the basis of the NPC during the remainder of FY98. Beginning in FY99, the NPC became an office of the Commerce Department. The Office of Personnel Management provides the necessary assistance in facilitating the NPC's operations. The NPC will terminate at the end of FY2001, unless extended by Presidential directive.

National Infrastructure Protection Center (NIPC)

As part of a national warning and information sharing system, the President immediately authorized the FBI to expand its current organization to a full scale National Infrastructure Protection Center (NIPC). This organization was tasked with serving as a national critical infrastructure threat assessment, warning, vulnerability, and law enforcement investigation and response entity. It included FBI, USSS, and other investigators experienced in computer crimes and infrastructure protection, as well as representatives detailed from the Department of Defense, the intelligence community, and lead agencies. It will be linked electronically to the rest of the federal government, including other warning and operations centers, as well as any private sector sharing and analysis centers. Its mission includes providing timely warnings of intentional threats, comprehensive analyses and law enforcement investigation and response.

All executive departments and agencies were directed to cooperate with the NIPC and provide such assistance, information, and advice as the NIPC requested to the extent permitted by law. All executive departments were directed to share with the NIPC information about threats and warning of attacks and about actual attacks on critical government and private sector infrastructures to the extent permitted by law. The NIPC incorporates elements responsible for warning, analysis, computer investigation, coordinating emergency response, training, outreach and development, and application of technical tools. In addition, it is developing its own relations directly with others in the private sector and with any information sharing and analysis entity that the private sector may create, such as the Information Sharing and Analysis Center described below.

The NIPC, in conjunction with the information originating agency, was to sanitize law enforcement and intelligence information for inclusion into analyses and reports that it will provide, in appropriate form, to relevant federal, state, and local agencies; the relevant owners and operators of critical infrastructures; and to any private sector information sharing and analysis entity. Before disseminating national security or other information that originated from the intelligence community, the NIPC was to coordinate fully with the intelligence community through existing procedures

The NIPC was directed to issue attack warnings or alerts to increases in threat condition to any private sector information sharing and analysis entity and to the owners and operators. These warnings were to include guidance regarding additional protection measures to be taken by owners and operators. Except in extreme emergencies, the NIPC is to coordinate with the National Coordinator before issuing public warnings of imminent attacks by international terrorists, foreign states, or other malevolent foreign powers. Finally, the NIPC was directed to provide a national focal point for gathering information on threats to the infrastructures. Additionally, the NIPC was to provide the principal means of facilitating and coordinating the federal government's response to an incident, mitigating attacks, investigating threats, and monitoring reconstitution efforts.

Information Sharing and Analysis Center (ISAC)

The National Coordinator, working with sector coordinators, sector liaison officials, and the National Economic Council, shall consult with owners and operators of the critical infrastructures to strongly encourage the creation of a private sector information sharing and analysis center or Information Sharing and Analysis Center (ISAC): The actual design and functions of the center and its relation to the NIPC were to be determined by the private sector, in consultation with and with assistance from the federal government. The center was to serve as the mechanism for gathering, analyzing, appropriately sanitizing, and disseminating private sector information to both industry and the NIPC.

The center was also to gather, analyze, and disseminate information from the NIPC for further distribution to the private sector. While crucial to a successful government-industry partnership, this mechanism for sharing important information about vulnerabilities, threats, intrusions, and anomalies is not to interfere with direct information exchanges between companies and the government. It was to establish baseline statistics and patterns on the various infrastructures, become a clearinghouse for information within and among the various sectors, and provide a library for historical data to be used by the private sector and, as deemed appropriate by the ISAC, by the government. Critical to the success of such an institution would be its timeliness, accessibility, co-ordination, flexibility, utility, and acceptability.

National Infrastructure Assurance Council

PPD-63 established a National Infrastructure Assurance Council. On the recommendation of the lead agencies, the National Economic Council and the National Coordinator, the President appointed a panel of major infrastructure providers and state and local government officials to serve as the National Infrastructure Assurance Council. The President appoints the chairman and the National Coordinator serves as the council's executive director. The National Infrastructure Assurance Council will meet periodically to enhance the partnership of the public and private sectors in protecting our critical infrastructures and will provide reports to the President as appropriate. Senior federal government officials will participate in the meetings of the National Infrastructure Assurance Council as appropriate.

To protect the federal government's own critical infrastructures, President Clinton ordered that "every department and agency shall develop a plan for protecting its own critical infrastructure, including but not limited to its cyber-based systems." Every department and agency of the federal government was made responsible for protecting its own critical infrastructure, especially its cyber-based systems. Every department and agency chief information officer (CIO) shall be responsible for information assurance. Every department and agency shall appoint a chief infrastructure assurance officer (CIAO) who shall be responsible for the protection of all of the other aspects of that department's critical infrastructure. These officials were to establish procedures for obtaining expedient and valid authorizations to allow vulnerability assessments to be performed on government computer and physical systems. The Department of Justice was to establish legal guidelines for providing for such authorizations.

The National Coordinator was made responsible for coordinating analyses required by the departments and agencies of inter-governmental dependencies and the mitigation of those dependencies. The Critical Infrastructure Coordination Group (CICG) was tasked with sponsoring an expert review process for those plans. No later than two years from today, those plans shall have been implemented and shall be updated every two years. In meeting this schedule, the federal government shall present a model to the private sector on how best to protect critical infrastructure.

National Infrastructure Assurance Plan

The principals committee was also tasked with creating a National Infrastructure Assurance Plan with milestones for accomplishing the following subordinate and related tasks.

- Vulnerability Analyses: For each sector of the economy and each sector of the government that might be a target of infrastructure attack intended to significantly damage the U.S., there shall be an initial vulnerability assessment, followed by periodic updates. As appropriate, these assessments shall also include the determination of the minimum essential infrastructure in each sector.

- Remedial Plan: Based upon the vulnerability assessment, there shall be a recommended remedial plan. The plan shall identify timelines for implementation, responsibilities, and funding.

- Warning: A national center to warn of significant infrastructure attacks will be established immediately (see Annex A). As soon thereafter as possible, we will put in place an enhanced system for detecting and analyzing such attacks, with maximum possible participation of the private sector.

- Response: A system shall develop a system for responding to a significant infrastructure attack while it is underway, with the goal of isolating and minimizing damage.

- Reconstitution: For varying levels of successful infrastructure attacks, we shall have a system to reconstitute minimum required capabilities rapidly.

- Education and Awareness: There shall be vulnerability awareness and education programs within both the government and the private sector to sensitize people regarding the importance of security and to train them in security standards, particularly regarding cyber-systems.

- Research and Development: Federally sponsored research and development in support of infrastructure protection shall be coordinated, be subject to multi-year planning, take into account private sector research, and be adequately funded to minimize our vulnerabilities on a rapid but achievable timetable.

- Intelligence: The intelligence community shall develop and implement a plan for enhancing collection and analysis of the foreign threat to our national infrastructure, to include but not be limited to the foreign cyber/information warfare threat.

- International Cooperation: There shall be a plan to expand cooperation on critical infrastructure protection with like-minded and friendly nations, international organizations, and multinational corporations.

- Legislative and Budgetary Requirements: There shall be an evaluation of the executive branch's legislative authorities and budgetary priorities regarding critical infrastructure, and ameliorative recommendations shall be made to the President as necessary. The evaluations and recommendations, if any, shall be coordinated with the Director of OMB.

Studies and Research

PDD-63 recognized that there were many areas where the federal government lacked the information to develop an effective critical infrastructure program. It directed the National Coordinator to commission studies on a wide range of legal and regulatory issues:

- Liability issues arising from participation by private sector companies in the information sharing process.
- Existing legal impediments to information sharing, with an eye to proposals to remove these impediments, including through the drafting of model codes in cooperation with the American Legal Institute.
- The necessity of document and information classification and the impact of such classification on useful dissemination, as well as the methods and information systems by which threat and vulnerability information can be shared securely while avoiding disclosure or unacceptable risk of disclosure to those who will misuse it.
- The improved protection, including secure dissemination and information handling systems, of industry trade secrets and other confidential business data, law enforcement information and evidentiary material, classified national security information, unclassified material disclosing vulnerabilities of privately owned infrastructures and apparently innocuous information that, in the aggregate, it is unwise to disclose.
- The implications of sharing information with foreign entities where such sharing is deemed necessary to the security of U.S. infrastructures. The potential benefit to security standards of mandating, subsidizing, or otherwise assisting in the provision of insurance for selected critical infrastructure providers and requiring insurance tie-ins for foreign critical infrastructure providers hoping to do business with the U.S.

At the same time, it called for much broader studies and reviews of actions within the federal government:

- The intelligence community shall elevate and formalize the priority for enhanced collection and analysis of information on the foreign cyber/information warfare threat to our critical infrastructure.
- The Federal Bureau of Investigation, the Secret Service, and other appropriate agencies shall: (1) vigorously recruit undergraduate and graduate students with the relevant computer-related technical skills for full-time employment as well as for part-time work with regional computer crime

squads; and (2) facilitate the hiring and retention of qualified personnel for technical analysis and investigation involving cyber-attacks.

- The Department of Transportation, in consultation with the Department of Defense, shall undertake a thorough evaluation of the vulnerability of the national transportation infrastructure that relies on the Global Positioning System (GPS). This evaluation shall include sponsoring an independent, integrated assessment of risks to civilian users of GPS-based systems, with a view to basing decisions on the ultimate architecture of the modernized NAS on these evaluations.

- The Federal Aviation Administration shall develop and implement a comprehensive National Airspace System Security Program to protect the modernized NAS from information-based and other disruptions and attacks.

- GSA shall identify large procurements (such as the new Federal Telecommunications System, FTS 2000) related to infrastructure assurance, study whether the procurement process reflects the importance of infrastructure protection and propose, if necessary, revisions to the overall procurement process to do so.

- OMB shall direct federal agencies to include assigned infrastructure assurance functions within their Government Performance and Results Act strategic planning and performance measurement framework.

- The NSA, in accordance with its National Manager responsibilities in NSD-42, shall provide assessments encompassing examinations of U.S. government systems to interception and exploitation; disseminate threat and vulnerability information; establish standards; conduct research and development; and conduct issue security product evaluations.

Cooperation with the Private and Civil Sectors

PDD-63 called for the federal government to steadily expand the scope of its efforts to work with the private sector and recognized that such cooperation is essential to information and critical infrastructure protection. In contrast, the earlier computer security, paperwork reduction, and Clinger-Cohen Act had focused on government systems.

In order to assist the private sector in achieving and maintaining infrastructure security, PDD-63 directed the National Coordinator and the National Infrastructure Assurance Council should propose and develop ways to encourage private industry to perform periodic risk assessments of critical processes, including information and telecommunications systems. It also stated that:

- The Department of Commerce and the Department of Defense shall work together, in coordination with the private sector, to offer their expertise to private owners and operators of critical infrastructure to develop security-related best practice standards.

- The Department of Justice and Department of the Treasury shall sponsor a comprehensive study compiling demographics of computer crime, comparing state approaches to computer crime, and developing ways of deterring and responding to computer crime by juveniles.

PDD-63 recognized that many private information systems are at least as important to America's economy and civil society as the vast majority of federal, state, and local government systems. Both the government and private industry have information systems, storage, and technology that are essential to the operation of critical infrastructure. What is not clear is what role government should play in aiding the private and civil sectors and how much responsibility must devolve on given users and consumers in dealing with given levels of attack.

PDD-63 also recognized the need to foster a climate of enhanced public sensitivity to the problem of infrastructure protection and for an outreach program. It directed that the following actions be taken:

- The White House, under the oversight of the National Coordinator, together with the relevant Cabinet agencies shall consider a series of conferences: (1) that will bring together national leaders in the public and private sectors to propose programs to increase the commitment to information security; (2) that convoke academic leaders from engineering, computer science, business, and law schools to review the status of education in information security and will identify changes in the curricula and resources necessary to meet the national demand for professionals in this field; (3) on the issues around computer ethics as these relate to the K through 12 and general university populations.

- The National Academy of Sciences and the National Academy of Engineering shall consider a round table bringing together federal, state, and local officials with industry and academic leaders to develop national strategies for enhancing infrastructure security.

- The intelligence community and law enforcement shall expand existing programs for briefing infrastructure owners and operators and senior government officials.

- The National Coordinator shall (1) establish a program for infrastructure assurance simulations involving senior public and private officials, the reports of which might be distributed as part of an awareness campaign; and (2) in coordination with the private sector, launch a continuing national awareness campaign, emphasizing improving infrastructure security.

Annual Report on Implementation

Finally, the National Coordinator, working with the National Economic Council, was tasked with providing an annual report on the implementation of this directive to the President and the heads of departments and agencies, through the Assistant to the President for National Security Affairs. The report was to include an updated threat assessment, a status report on achieving the milestones identified for the national plan and additional policy, legislative, and budgetary recommendations. The evaluations and recommendations were to be coordinated with the director of OMB.

NATIONAL PLAN FOR INFORMATION
SYSTEMS PROTECTION

As a result of PDD-63, the first National Plan for Information Systems Protection was released on January 7, 2000. This National Plan summarized the progress to date and issued a more complete plan for the protection of information systems which laid out specific measures to be taken to both "prepare and prevent" and "detect and respond" to information system attacks. The plan also reiterated the connection between providing better information security and protecting critical infrastructures.

National Plan for Information Systems Protection, Version One

The "National Plan for Information Systems Protection, Version One" called for "the establishment of the U.S. government as a model of information security, and the development of a public-private partnership to defend our national infrastructures."[47] The White House fact sheet the administration issued along with the plan stated that funding on critical infrastructure would increase by 16 percent in the FY 2001 budget proposal to $2.03 billion. It also outlined the following key initiatives to protect the federal government's computer systems that had been developed and provided full or pilot funding:

- *Working to Recruit, Train, and Retain Federal IT Experts.* We have developed and provided FY2001 funding for a Federal Cyber Services Training and Education initiative led by OPM and NSF which calls for two programs: the first is an ROTC-like program where we pay for IT education (B.S. or M.S.) in exchange for federal service; and the second is a program to establish competencies and certify our existing IT workforce. ($25 million)
- *Conducting Federal Agency Vulnerability Analyses and Developing Agency CIP Plans.* Federal agencies have all developed CIP plans, and these have been reviewed by a newly created "Expert Review Team" (ERT) of federal

computer security experts. We have also established the ERT as a permanent team (at the Commerce Department's NIST), with funding lines in
FY2000 and 2001. ($5 million)

- *Designing a Federal Intrusion Detection Network (FIDNET).* To protect
  vital systems in federal civilian agencies, we are providing funding for
  development of a cyber-"burglar alarm" which alerts the federal government to cyber-attacks, provides recommended defenses, establishes information security readiness levels, and ensures the rapid implementation of
  system "patches" for known software defects. ($10 million)

- *Piloting Public Key Infrastructure Models.* The Clinton Administration is
  funding seven PKI pilot programs in FY2001 at different federal agencies.
  ($7 million)

- *Developing Federal R&D Efforts.* In addition to the Institute, we have
  worked to ensure that R&D investments in computer security will grow
  more than 35% in the FY2001 budget. ($621 million)

- *Building the Public-Private Partnership.* The President is committed to
  building partnerships with the private sector to protect our computer networks through the following initiatives:

- *Institute for Information Infrastructure Protection.* Building on a Science
  Advisory Panel, we are proposing to create an Information Infrastructure
  Institute which would combine federal and private sector energies to fill
  the gaps in critical infrastructure R&D that are not now being met in the
  private sector or the Department of Defense. It would also provide dem-
  onstration and development support in key areas like benchmarks and
  standards and curriculum development. ($50m)

- *Partnership for Critical Infrastructure Security.* This alliance of more than
  ninety Fortune 500 companies is spearheaded by Secretary Daley and had
  a successful kickoff in New York on December 8th. We will build on this
  partnership to provide public education and cooperation with the private
  sector on a wide variety of information security issues.

- *Information Sharing and Analysis Centers (ISACs).* Two of the proposed
  six private sector computer security centers have been established (banking and finance and telecommunications). The other four sectors are being worked with to get their proposed ISACs operational.

- *National Infrastructure Assurance Council.* The President signed an Executive Order creating this advisory council last year. Its members are now
  being recruited from senior ranks of the IT industry, key sectors of the
  corporate economy, and academia.

The plan stated that the Clinton Administration intended to reach an
initial operating capacity. "Full capability" was defined as the capability to fulfill the goal of PDD-63 to the point where any disruption of

information and critical infrastructures would be "brief, infrequent, manageable, geographically isolated, and minimally detrimental to the welfare of the U.S." The plan set forth three objectives: *prepare and prevent* successful attacks on critical infrastructures, *detect and respond,* to *assess and contain* attacks quickly, and to *build strong foundations.*[48] Ten programs were included in the plan to achieve these objectives.[49]

- Prepare and Prevent Program 1: Identify critical infrastructure assets and shared interdependencies and address vulnerabilities.
- Detect and Respond Program 2: Detect attacks and unauthorized intrusions.
- Program 3: Develop robust intelligence and law enforcement capabilities to protect critical information systems consistent with the law.
- Program 4: Share attack warnings and information in a timely manner.
- Program 5: Create capabilities for response, reconstitution, and recovery.
- Program 6: Enhance research and development in support of programs 1–5.
- Program 7: Train and employ adequate numbers of information security specialists.
- Program 8: Outreach to make Americans aware of the need for improved cyber-security.
- Program 9: Adopt legislation and appropriations in support of programs 1–8.
- Program 10: In every step and component of the plan, ensure the full protection of American citizens' civil liberties, their rights to privacy, and their rights to protection of proprietary data.

GAO Comments on the National Plan for Information Systems Protection

Inevitably, neither the plan nor federal implementation efforts achieved all of their goals. Jack L. Brock, Jr., director of government-wide and Defense Information Systems Accounting and Information Management Division of General Accounting Office (GAO) made a detailed critique of the first National Plan in testimony before the Senate Subcommittee on Technology, Terrorism, and Government Information on February 1, 2000. He praised the plan as an "important and positive step forward toward building the cyber-defense necessary to protect critical information assets and infrastructures." He also, however, raised points where the plan could be improved and called for a greater emphasis on computer security and the need to rely less on "outmoded" legislation and requirements which he felt were poorly implemented.[50]

The GAO's criticisms focused on several of the plan's recommendations. The GAO questioned whether or not making the federal government a model of good information security is feasible, especially considering the gap between expectations and agency performance. If the government cannot meet its own expectations then how can it become a model for the public? Brock's testimony stated that GAO audits had found that even the most basic controls, such as overly broad access privileges, were repeatedly violated. The government failures were said to be the result of poor security management.[51]

As for clarifying defined roles and responsibilities, the GAO acknowledged that the plan made progress in this area by "better defining the critical infrastructure protection responsibilities of the many federal entities involved" and formalizing "a number of new entities, interagency working groups, and projects that will have to be integrated into the existing framework of computer security activities."[52] Brock then reiterated the GAO's call for strong leadership to coordinate information security issues.

Brock went on to discuss GAO's recommendations for risk-based standards, routine evaluations of agency performance, executive branch and congressional oversight, the need for technical expertise and proper funding, the importance of incident detection and response, legislative framework, and engaging public–private partnerships. All of these are discussed at length in Brock's statement:[53]

> This plan calls for new initiatives to strengthen the nation's defenses against threats to public and private sector information systems that are critical to the country's economic and social welfare, particularly those supporting public utilities, telecommunications, finance, emergency services, and government operations. As a "preliminary" document, it is intended to begin a dialogue on its proposals and lead to the development of plans for protecting other elements of the nation's infrastructure, including those pertaining to the physical infrastructure and specific roles and responsibilities for state and local governments and the private sector.
>
> Beginning this dialogue is vital. As I stressed at this subcommittee's October 1999 hearing on critical infrastructure protection, our nation's computer-based infrastructures are at increasing risk of severe disruption. The dramatic increase of computer interconnectivity—while facilitating communications, business processes, and access to information—has increased the risk that problems affecting one system will also affect other interconnected systems. Massive computer networks provide pathways among

systems that, if not properly secured, can be used to gain unauthorized access to data and operations from remote locations. While the threats or sources of these problems can include natural disasters, such as earthquakes, and system-induced problems, government officials are increasingly concerned about attacks from individuals and groups with malicious intentions, such as terrorists and nations engaging in information warfare.

This plan is an important and positive step forward toward building the cyber-defense necessary to protect critical information assets and infrastructures.

- It identifies risks associated with our nation's dependence on computers and computer networks for critical services.
- It recognizes the need for the federal government to take the lead in addressing critical infrastructure risks and to serve as a model for information security.
- It outlines key concepts and general initiatives to assist in achieving these goals.

In doing this, the plan addresses many of the same points we raised at last October's hearing, including the need for improved standards, strengthened evaluations and oversight of agency performance, increased technical expertise, adequate funding, and improved incident detection and response capabilities.

However, there are opportunities for improvement as the plan is further developed as well as significant challenges that must be addressed to build the public–private partnerships necessary for infrastructure protection. In particular, we believe the plan should place more emphasis on providing agencies the incentives and tools to implement the management controls necessary to assure comprehensive computer security programs, as opposed to its current strong emphasis on implementing intrusion detection capabilities. In addition, the plan relies heavily on legislation and requirements already in place that, as a whole, are outmoded and inadequate as well as poorly implemented by the agencies.

Mr. Chairman, my testimony today will provide a more detailed overview of the plan, identify opportunities for sharpening the plan's proposals for improving the federal government's security programs, and outline the challenges facing the government in building the public–private partnerships necessary for comprehensive infrastructure protections.

Overview of the National Plan for Information Systems Protection

The plan proposes achieving its twin goals of making the U.S. government a model of information security and developing a public–private partnership to defend our national infrastructure through the following ten programs which are intended to serve three crosscutting infrastructure protection objectives.

Crosscutting Objectives	Program
Prepare and Prevent	
The steps necessary to minimize the possibility of significant and successful attack on our critical information networks, and build an infrastructure that remains effective in the face of such attacks.	Identify critical infrastructure assests and shared interdependencies and address vulnerabilities.
Detect and Respond	
The actions required to identify and assess an attack in a timely way, and then to contain the attack, quickly recover from it, and reconstitute affected systems.	Detect attacks and unauthorized intrusions. Develop intelligence and law enforcement capabilities to protect critical information systems. Share attack warning and information in a timely manner. Create capabilities for response, reconstitution, and recovery.
Build Strong Foundations	
The steps needed to create and nourish the people, organizations, laws, and traditions that will make us better able to prepare for and prevent, detect, and respond to attacks on our critical information networks.	Enhance research and development. Train and employ adequate numbers of information security specialists. Outreach to make Americans aware of the need for improved cyber-security. Adopt legislation and appropriations to support infrastructure protections. Ensure the full protection of American civil liberties, their rights to privacy, and their rights to the protection of proprietary data.

Making the Federal Government a Model

Making the federal government a model of good information security is essential to the plan's success. However, the gap between expectations and actual agency performance is significant. As we testified last October and in subsequent written responses to your questions, our government is not adequately protecting critical federal operations and assets from computer-based attacks. In particular, recent audits conducted by GAO and agency inspectors general show that 22 of the largest federal agencies have significant computer security weaknesses, ranging from poor controls over access to sensitive systems and data, to poor control over software development and changes, and nonexistent or weak continuity of service plans.

Importantly, our audits have repeatedly identified serious deficiencies in the most basic controls over access to federal systems. For example, managers often provided overly broad access privileges to very large groups of users, affording far more individuals than necessary the ability to browse, and sometimes, modify or delete sensitive or critical information.

In addition, access was often not appropriately authorized or documented; users often shared accounts and passwords or posted passwords in plain view; software access controls were improperly implemented; and user activity was not adequately monitored to deter and identify inappropriate actions.

While a number of factors have contributed to weak federal information security, such as insufficient understanding of risks, technical staff shortages, and a lack of system and security architectures, the fundamental underlying problem is poor security program management. As we reported in 1996 and, again, in 1998, agencies have not established security management programs to ensure that controls, once implemented properly, are effective on an ongoing basis. This framework of effective access controls and management oversight is fundamental to any good computer security program.

At last October's hearing, we also observed that other crosscutting actions—ranging from clarifying the roles and responsibilities of the many entities involved in information security, to strengthening oversight, to securing adequate technical expertise and funding—were needed in seven key areas to provide greater assurance that critical infrastructure objectives can be met. I would like to discuss how the plan addresses each of these areas and what additional actions need to be taken.

Clearly Defined Roles and Responsibilities

The plan takes some positive steps to resolve this problem. For example, it discusses in very general terms how tasks associated with accomplishing the plan's objectives relate to computer security responsibilities outlined in existing laws and related guidance. These include the federal computer security and information resource management responsibilities of OMB, agency chief information officers, chief financial officers as well as the CIO council. It describes OMB's core responsibility for managing federal computer security and information technology. And it generally defines the roles of the major entities created by PDD-63, including the National Coordinator for Security, Infrastructure Protection and Counterterrorism, the Critical Infrastructure Assurance Office, and the National Infrastructure Protection Center.

In this regard, the plan makes a start at better defining the critical infrastructure protection responsibilities of the many federal entities involved. The plan also introduces or formalizes a number of new entities, interagency working groups, and projects that will have to be integrated into the existing framework of computer security activities. Examples of these new entities and efforts include an expert review team for evaluating agency infrastructure protection plans, a federal intrusion detection network, and an interagency working group on system security practices. Because of the number of entities involved (some established by law, some by executive order, and others with less formal mandates), strong and effective leadership will be essential to ensure that their efforts are coordinated and adequately communicated to individual agency personnel and that critical infrastructure protection efforts are appropriately linked with broader computer security efforts.

Risk-Based Standards

Currently, agencies have wide discretion in deciding (1) what computer controls to implement and (2) the level of rigor with which to enforce these controls. In theory, this is appropriate since, as OMB and NIST guidance states, the level of protection provided should be commensurate with the related risk to operations and assets. In security, one size does not fit all. The risks associated with different types of data and operations vary, depending on their sensitivity and criticality. For example, for undercover law enforcement operations, data confidentiality must be protected at all cost, while for other types of data, such as current information on financial markets, data integrity is the uppermost concern.

Our audit work has shown that agencies have generally done a very poor job of evaluating their information security risks and implementing appropriate controls. As a result, we believe that more specific guidance on what types of controls are appropriate for specific types of systems and data and the ways in which these controls should be implemented would be helpful. Specifically, a more prescriptive set of control standards, supported by a range of data classifications and related minimum requirements, would help clarify expectations for information protection, provide a framework for assessing information security risk, and help ensure that similar types of data and shared data are provided the same level of protection from one agency to another. In essence, risk-based standards would assist agencies in ensuring that their most critical operations and assets are protected at the highest levels, while providing agencies the flexibility to apply less rigorous (and often less expensive and less cumbersome) controls to lower-risk operations and assets.

Routine Evaluations of Agency Performance

The plan takes some constructive steps in this regard. Particularly, it calls on federal agencies to put in place programs to carry out several types of vulnerability testing and analysis, including routine automated system configuration/integrity/vulnerability testing using commercial-off-the-shelf tools, regular internal self-assessments, and independent external critical reviews. At an agency's request, NSA and NIST are to perform independent analyses of critical federal information infrastructure and provide independent reports of their results to the agency's CIO. And, as mentioned earlier, the plan anticipates establishing a permanent Expert Review Team at NIST to assist government-wide agencies in adhering to federal computer security requirements.

Nevertheless, we believe that the plan's provisions for testing agency controls may not be rigorous enough. Tests initiated by agency officials are essential because they provide information needed to fulfill their ongoing responsibility for managing security programs. However, routine in-depth tests and evaluations initiated by independent auditors, such as agency inspectors general, are also critical because they serve as an independent check on management evaluations and provide reliable information on actual control effectiveness for congressional and executive branch oversight.

Our audits at individual agencies and our best practices work have shown that a continuous cycle of testing, reassessment of risk, and adjustments to policies and controls is needed to ensure that efforts to protect information remain appropriate and effective on an ongoing basis. Establishing such a cycle of activity will require a significant commitment by agency management, the federal audit community, and federal centers of technical expertise, such as NSA and NIST. It will be important for any new audit requirements, including those associated with the Expert Review Team, to be conducted in this context.

Executive Branch and Congressional Oversight

The administration's call to action through this plan's development and increased congressional interest indicates a heightened concern over cybersecurity and provides a basis for increased oversight. As noted in the previous section, initial oversight must provide a heavy focus on agency management's fulfillment of its obligations to set and evaluate meaningful controls over its information environment.

Adequate Technical Expertise

The plan does a good job of addressing this issue. It describes a program to develop a cadre of highly skilled computer science and information security personnel. This program, if implemented, would include estimating personnel and training needs; establishing centers for information technology excellence that will provide Web-based and classroom information security training to federal employees, college and high school students; initiating a scholarship program under which recipients would agree to a pre-determined commitment to federal government service; and establishing a high school and secondary school outreach program.

Adequate Funding

In releasing the plan on January 7, the President announced that he was proposing a 16 percent increase in funding for critical infrastructure protection in his fiscal year 2001 budget proposal. To jumpstart fiscal year 01 initiatives, the President also proposed $9 million in supplemental funding for this spring.

We have not had the opportunity to examine this proposal in detail. However, as this plan evolves, it will be important to secure OMB and congressional oversight of spending in order to ensure that expenditures are targeted toward reducing the most significant risks and that controls implemented are effective. Our audits have shown that, in the past, agencies have expended resources on controls that, when tested, proved to be ineffective. In addition, they have often addressed identified weaknesses in an ad hoc, piecemeal fashion that resulted in limited improvement. It will be important for future security budgets to be based primarily on risk-based needs and for expenditures to be evaluated, to the extent possible, in terms of actual risk reduction.

Incident Detection and Response

The plan proposes to strengthen incident detection and response by developing mechanisms for regular sharing of federal threats, vulnerability, and warning data; and sponsoring conferences to further the coordination and development of common operating systems. In particular, it calls for a government-wide system for analyzing and correlating attack data consisting of three elements: one for the Department of Defense and national security communities (the Joint Task Force-Computer Network Defense, which is already deployed), a second for non-Defense federal departments and agencies (the Federal Intrusion Detection Network, or FIDNet which will build on existing DoD and other security technology expertise), and a third that provides information to both systems (the National Security Incident Response Center, or NSIRC, which has already been deployed to provide expert assistance to the national security community in isolating, containing, and resolving incidents threatening national security systems).

We agree that developing improved intrusion detection and response capabilities is important. However, available tools and methods for analyzing network traffic and detecting intrusions are still evolving and cannot yet be relied on to serve as an effective "burglar alarm," as envisioned by the plan. While holding promise for the future, such tools and methods currently raise many questions regarding technical feasibility, cost-effectiveness, and the appropriate extent of centralized federal oversight. Accordingly, these efforts merit close congressional oversight.

Legislative Framework

At present, there is legislation pending in both Houses that seeks to correct some of these underlying deficiencies. Among other things, these proposals call for a more comprehensive framework for establishing and ensuring the effectiveness of controls over information resources that support federal operations and assets; recognize the highly networked nature of the federal computing environment; and provide better oversight mechanisms. Such efforts could play an integral role in further strengthening the plan.

Engaging Public–Private Partnerships

For instance, the plan seeks to establish a Partnership for Critical Infrastructure Security and a National Infrastructure Assurance Council to increase corporate and government communications about shared threats to critical information systems. It also proposes establishing Information Sharing and Analysis Centers to facilitate public–private sector information sharing about actual threats and vulnerabilities in individual infrastructure sectors. These, as well as other proposals, however, are presented in broad terms, with the intent that future versions of the plan will describe a full spectrum of specific actions and programs that have been jointly agreed upon by industry and all levels of government.

We believe this approach is reasonable given the formidable challenges involved in developing effective partnerships with the private sector. The plan itself recognizes some of these challenges. For example, it acknowledges that critical infrastructure protection is not exclusively, even largely, within the province of the federal government, and, as a result, the federal government is limited in what it can do to protect critical infrastructures. It also recognizes that while the nature of the threat to our national infrastructure has changed, the true extent of that threat, our vulnerability to it, and possible means of defense are not entirely clear. Furthermore, the plan appreciates that solutions to critical infrastructure protection must be tailored sector by sector, through consultation about vulnerabilities, threats, and possible response strategies.

At the same time the plan recognizes such challenges, it proposes several initiatives that may have a significant impact on the private sector and affected interest groups. For example, the plan raises the possibility of reviewing laws for possible amendments to remove barriers that discourage private sector companies from sharing information with government agencies about infrastructure protection issues. Specifically, it raises the idea of more explicit confidentiality protections (so that federal law enforcement or defense agencies could assure private companies that such information would not be accessible through the Freedom of Information Act) as well as changes to antitrust or tort liability laws. Because such changes could involve important tradeoffs among significant policy concerns as well as affected interest groups, it will be important to proceed carefully in addressing the concerns of affected parties while at the same time providing the incentives needed to garner private sector cooperation.

The plan also suggests increasing employer rights to monitor employees. This would provide one means of protecting organizations from the "insiders," who as a practical matter, probably pose a greater threat to organizational security than do external threats. Again, the challenge will lie in balancing individual privacy concerns with the need to protect sensitive assets and the common welfare.

These are just two examples of possible changes that may have the potential of improving the public–private partnership for information protection, but that will require extensive public dialogue before they could or should be implemented.

Mr. Chairman, this concludes my statement. The plan fulfills the commitment made on its title page: it does invite a meaningful dialogue. The plan is an engaging step forward in improving the nation's cyber-infrastructure. As noted in the statement, much more needs to be done to strengthen the plan's ambitious goal of making the government a model. And serious consideration of changes in the computer security legislative framework is necessary to better assure agency compliance with good practice and process. Finally, the challenges facing the establishment of a meaningful public-private partnership require a level of continuous, long-term commitment on all sides that will be difficult to sustain but that are certainly achievable.

Oplan 3600

Little official data is available on U.S. plans for cyber-warfare and on the offensive capabilities of the Defense Department and intelligence community. At a conference on National Strategies and Capabilities for a Changing World in November 2000, however, public reference was made to a U.S. plan for cyber-attack. Lt. General Edward Anderson, deputy commander in chief at U.S. Space Command, spoke of a plan called Oplan 3600, which he said was backed by President Clinton and Secretary of Defense Cohen.

He indicated that Oplan 3600 would be the first U.S. military cyber-attack strategy. It is designed by the U.S. Space Command, and the "strategy would detail actions to be followed by the Unified Commander in Chief (CINC) if the president and the secretary of defense order a cyber-strike." Such a response could consist of denial of service strikes, sending out viruses, and jamming of enemy information systems. Anderson said he believed that other countries, such as Israel, China, and Russia, were already developing information warfare attack plans.[54]

THE SUCCESS OF THE FEDERAL GOVERNMENT
EFFORT TO DATE

Taken at face value, the U.S. government has made major progress in the last decade, and particularly since issuing PDD-63. At the same time, major gaps seem to remain between its efforts to deal with cyber-warfare and lower levels of cyber-attack. There has been no coordinated public effort to set clear milestones and measures of effectiveness and report on progress to date. Both praise and criticism tend to be anecdotal and focus on policy, tasking, and organizational responsibilities—rather than actual progress in improving given aspects of critical infrastructure protection.

At this writing it is unclear whether the Bush Administration will be any more successful in coming to grips with these realities than the Clinton Administration was. The new administration will not be able to shape any comprehensive approach to planning, programming, and budgeting before it submits its FY2003 budget in early 2002, and it is unclear that it will be able to really formulate a comprehensive program before its FY2004 budget submission. Like the Clinton Administration, the Bush Administration has given information warfare and critical infrastructure protection high priority in its public statements. It has also begun to conduct the almost inevitable reorganization of U.S. government efforts, which seems to be the first step of every major shift in political control of the White House. As yet, however, it has done little to actually plan, budget, or manage, or to create a clear set of overall priorities for the U.S. government, for state and local action, and for private sector NGOs.

As is the case with virtually all federal program descriptions and justifications, there is no future year program, as distinguished from annual programs and budget justifications. The longer term goals for federal action are not made public, even at the agency or departmental level. No department or agency sets even mid-term goals for any given activity or program, or provides any data on the longer term procurement and life cycle costs of creating an effective program. The vulnerabilities of the federal effort, and the cost and technical ability to defeat key components are not identified. No effort is made to provide a net assessment of current capabilities relative to threats, or technological net assessment of how this situation will change over time. There also are no clear benchmarks of what level of cooperation has been achieved with state and local governments or with the private and civil sectors.

The resulting problems can only be analyzed in part by a review of the efforts of individual departments and agencies, and little hard data is available on many aspects of the defense and intelligence effort. It is virtually impossible to do more than speculate on whether federal efforts are catching up with the increase in the potential threat, are adequate to deal with ongoing and probable changes in technology, or are matched by suitable efforts at other levels of government and in the private sector.

Somewhat ironically, the phrase "management information systems" seems to be something of an oxymoron when it comes to transparency as to the details of what the government has or has not accomplished and plans to do in the future. In fairness, there may be "management" and there may be "systems," but there is little concrete "information" to show it.

Chapter 4

Analyzing Federal Critical Infrastructure Programs by Department and Agency

There is no clear way to cost the federal critical infrastructure program, and only speculative data seems to be available on the efforts being made at the state and local levels, and by the private and civil sector. In the case of governments, there are great many law enforcement, intelligence, counterterrorism, and emergency response efforts that are not dedicated to critical infrastructure per se but which play an important role in shaping the nation's capabilities. The Department of Defense and intelligence community's offensive information warfare programs may have a powerful retaliatory and deterrent effect but are not part of the CIP program. At the same time, a number of departments and agencies seem to have recast programs to take advantage of the funding available as CIP funding, and some have blurred the line between ongoing MIS activity and CIP activity.

There are, however, two major sources of data on dedicated critical infrastructure programs and expenses. One is the National Plan for Information Systems Protection. The other is an analysis of the FY2001 budget performed by OMB. While these two analyses overlap, they both provide different insights into the federal effort, and define the issues the Bush Administration must now come to grips with.

THE NATIONAL PLAN FOR INFORMATION
SYSTEMS ESTIMATE

According to the National Plan for Information Systems Protection the FY2000 budget provided a $1.737 billion for government efforts to

Table 4.1
Funding for Critical Infrastructure Protection (in millions of dollars)

Agency	FY1998 Actual	FY1999 Actual	FY2000 Enacted
National Security	975	1,185	1,403
Treasury	23	49	76
NASA	41	43	66
Transportation	20	25	51
Justice	26	54	46
NSF	19	21	27
Commerce	9	22	18
HHS	22	12	13
Other	9	18	37
Total	1,144	1,429	1,737

Source: "National Plan for Information Systems Protection," p. 121.

protect critical infrastructure, a 20 percent or $300 million increase from FY1999. This budget included "funding for new programs to address key vulnerabilities, as well as for ongoing efforts to assure the security of interconnected infrastructures such as telecommunications, banking and finance, energy, transportation, and essential government services." These spending trends are summarized in Table 4.1

CIP spending is divided into three major headings: research and development, federal (non-national security) program operations, and national security program operations. These can be broken down into smaller program operations that encompass the following areas: vulnerability assessment, risk management, protection and mitigation, intrusion detection, incident response and reconstitution, and education and awareness.[55]

Government spending for CIP by sector weighs heavily in favor of government and emergency services as can be seen in Table 4.2.

The plan also provided the following description of how the funding is executed for the critical infrastructure sectors, the interdependency initiative, and ISACs.

- *Government and Emergency Services.* Funds for this sector increased by more than 20 percent over the previous budget, the majority of which support national defense agencies' efforts to protect critical infrastructures.

Table 4.2
Critical Infrastructure Spending by Sector (in millions of dollars)

	FY1998 Actual	FY1999 Actual	FY2000 Actual
Government and Emergency Services	1,042	1,282	1,565
Information and Communications	41	57	58
Transportation	25	32	57
Electric Power, Oil and Gas Production and Storage, and Water Supply	22	35	30
Banking and Finance	12	17	15
Interdependencies	0	0	8
Total	1,144	1,429	1,737

- *Information and Communications.* $33 million is provided to seven agencies for computer security research and development proposals.
- *Transportation.* To address Federal Aviation Administration facilities and information systems, and for programs to reduce vulnerabilities in the National Airspace System and surface transportation systems, the budget significantly increases funding for this sector from $32 million to $57 million.
- *Electric Power, Oil and Gas Production and Storage, and Water Supply.* The $30 million budgeted for this area supports ongoing programs in the Department of Energy, Department of Interior, and Environmental Protection Agency to advise energy companies and metropolitan water agencies in CIP planning, and for basic research. These efforts advance the goal of public-private partnerships to meet common CIP needs.
- *Banking and Finance.* The Treasury Department received $16 million to coordinate protection of critical facilities, equipment, and operations in the banking and finance sector. As directed by the PDD, Treasury actively leads sector CIP efforts as well as serving as a model for other sectors.
- *Interdependencies.* The budget provides $5 million to DoD, Commerce, and the National Science Foundation to study relationships among infrastructures, and to build up our capability to ensure a reliable, interconnected, and secure information system infrastructure.
- *Information Sharing and Analysis Centers.* $8 million for sector liaison lead agencies is provided in the budget to help establish Information Sharing and Analysis Centers (ISAC). ISACs are designed to foster private sector development and to share recommended practices and standards.

The plan also discussed the new initiatives that advance the goals of the Presidential Decision Directive to protect critical infrastructure. The initiatives listed below may support several critical infrastructure sectors. These initiatives represent only a portion of the total of the $1.737 billion CIP program.

- *Computer Security Research and Development Initiative.* $80 million is allocated for R&D to study safeguarding networks and databases, and detection of anomalous activities, "trap doors," Trojan Horses, and other malicious code.
- *Information Sharing and Analysis Centers.* As noted earlier, ISACs are designed to foster private sector development and share recommended practices and standards. $8 million is set aside in the budget to help establish ISACs.

In addition to these new programs, the plan continued to support the following ongoing efforts:

- *National Defense Infrastructure.* The budget increases resources to protect critical infrastructures that support national security requirements, bringing this funding to over $1.4 billion.
- *Federal Aviation Administration and National Airspace System.* FAA funding for CIP doubled, from $23 million to almost $50 million, to better protect FAA facilities and information systems, and for programs to reduce vulnerabilities in the National Airspace System.
- *Fighting Cyber-crime.* The budget provides $46 million to enhance the investigative and prosecutorial efforts of the FBI, the U.S. Attorney, and the Justice Department's Criminal Division.
- *Critical Infrastructure Assurance Office (CIAO).* The CIAO received $3 million to support efforts to develop a national infrastructure assurance plan and coordinate a national education and awareness program.

THE OMB ANALYSIS

OMB has found it difficult to create an accurate analysis of the budgetary data on CIP programs because of the lack of any clear definition of what programs should be included and the difficulties this has caused for the collection of data. The government is experiencing what the plan calls "a precipitous learning curve" in its attempts to provide consolidated data and adequate descriptions and data presentations. To deal with this matter the OMB and the National Security Council developed a process to review high-priority national security programs that cross agency lines. The process calls for program recommendations "being made on a government-wide context rather than agency by agency."

There are four phases in this new approach:[56]

- *Program Review*. Interagency working groups, chaired by the National Security Council or the Office of Science and Technology Policy, review the crosscutting issues in a government-wide context. The groups identify gaps and duplications in the national effort and develop detailed programmatic initiatives to increase our effectiveness in countering unconventional threats.

- *Budget Review*. For each issue area, a budget subgroup consisting of agency program staff, agency budget staff, and OMB examiners develop budget-quality cost estimates for the programmatic initiatives. This phase is not an endorsement of funding for the initiatives, but instead is an effort to provide realistic, well-justified cost estimates.

- *Agency Action on Recommendations*. The working groups then prioritize the initiatives and transmit them as funding recommendations to the agencies. Agencies will address the recommendations in the context of other priorities and fiscal constraints in their fall budget submissions to OMB.

- *Review of Agency Action*. OMB will review agency action on the recommendations and make any necessary course corrections in Passback based on information from the working groups, other agency priorities, and available resources.

These efforts to improve collection and analysis of CIP data were evident in the development of the President's proposed budget for FY2001. The process was completed under an accelerated schedule for the FY2001 budget, and will be used to develop the FY2002 budgets for crosscutting issues. Chart 4.1 depicts that schedule.

To expedite these efforts to improve data on CIP the process for the President's proposed budget for FY2001 were placed and completed under an accelerated schedule. Programmatic recommendations were to be completed by the end of March. The developments of IWG budget recommendations were to begin in March and be completed by the end of April. From May through July IWG recommendations were to be integrated into agency budgets. August through October agency actions were to be reviewed and October through December outstanding concerns were to be resolved.[57]

ANNUAL REPORT TO CONGRESS ON COMBATING TERRORISM

As required by Section 1050 of FY1998 National Defense Authorization Act, the administration provided information on Executive branch funding efforts to combat terrorism. Following legislation required an additional annex report on domestic preparedness.[58] The 2000 report combines information on programs funded to combat terrorism, enhance WMD preparedness, and protect critical infrastructures. The report also focused on the government wide review process launched in the National Plan for Information Systems Protection discussed in the aforementioned section.

It should be stressed, however, that the report does not include any aspects of offensive information and cyber-warfare that could be used to deter or respond to attacks. It also seems to omit any investment in designing less vulnerable systems and may ignore many investments in back-up or alternative systems. These problems are characteristic of all unclassified reporting on the nature and cost of federal critical infrastructure protection efforts.

According to the report the FY2001 budget calls for $2 billion for critical infrastructure protection/cybercrime.

> The budget proposes over $2 billion for critical infrastructure protection. These funds support a national effort to ensure the security of infrastructures in both the government and the private sector that are necessary to ensure our national security, national economic security, and public health and safety. The proposed funding for FY2001 represents a 15% increase over the FY2000 enacted level. It includes a 31% increase for R&D programs to develop the tools needed for effective infrastructure protection, bringing CIP R&D to a total $606 million. Of the total CIP budget, $1.7 billion protects Federal systems and ensures our ability to provide essential government services to the public. About $300 million fund agency efforts to provide assistance to the private sector, where most of the Nation's critical infrastructure resides.[59]

For information and telecommunication portions of infrastructure protection the report states that the administration has only begun encouraging "the operational changes necessary" for the protection of information systems. The report points to the National Plan for Information Systems Protection as the guide for both government protection of its own infrastructures and outreach to the private sector.[60]

> This sector is arguably the most critical in the CIP effort, because almost all other sectors depend to some extent on computers and other information networks. The administration has had considerable success in reaching out to industry associations to establish public/private partnerships and for input into our R&D agenda, but we have only begun to encourage the operational changes necessary for effective protection of this sector. The National Plan for Information Systems Protection is intended to provide strategic guidance for government protection of its own infrastructures as well as for outreach to the private sector. The administra-

tion is committed to implementing the plan in a manner so as to ensure consistency with other national policies, including privacy policies.

According to the report funding for CIP information systems protection has tripled since FY1998. This development is driven by the growth in R&D that has reached over $606 million in FY2001 mostly performed by the national security community.[61]

Government-wide Spending on CIP

The report separated out two main sectors of CIP spending, funding for protection of federal infrastructure, and funding for CIP assistance and outreach to the public sector. In FY2001 the latter made for 16 percent of the President's CIP budget, while funding for the protection of cyber and physical federal infrastructure makes up the lion's share. CIP assistance and public outreach includes funding for information and communications, banking and finance, transportation, energy, water supply, emergency services and interdependencies. Descriptions of sectors of particular interest are:

Government Services

As might be expected, most agency funding supports the protection of internal agency infrastructures. 84% of total CIP funding relates to government services. The administration has significantly increased investment in this area (increasing 65% since FY1998).[62]

Information and Communications

This sector is arguably the most critical in the CIP effort, because almost all other sectors depend to some extent on computers and other information networks. The administration has had considerable success in reaching out to industry associations to establish public/private partnerships for input into our R&D agenda, but we have only begun to encourage the operational changes necessary for effective protection of this sector. The National Plan for Information Systems Protection is intended to provide strategic guidance for government protection of its own infrastructures as well as outreach to the private sector. The administration is committed to implementing the plan in a manner as to ensure consistency with other national policies, including privacy policies.

Banking and Finance

We have made significant progress in the banking and finance sector because the industry is sensitive to this issue from its experience with cyber-crime. Treasury is the lead agency for outreach and assistance to this sector. In October 1999 the industry, with significant assistance from Treasure established an information sharing and analysis center (IASC) to facilitate exchange of warning and best practices information in this sector. Funding in this sector reflects Treasury Department activities for physical and cyber-protection of currency production, and Secret Service, Justice and FBI cyber-crime investigations.

Emergency Services

The Department of Justice/FBI is the lead agency for outreach and assistance to the emergency law enforcement service sector and is responsible for about half the funding for emergency services CIP. Justice funds efforts to address global computer crime and works with other agencies, the private sector, academic institutions, and foreign representatives to prevent, investigate, and prosecute computer terrorists. Justice improves the domestic and international infrastructure by providing assistance and advice to investigative agencies. FBI activities include prevention of attacks, computer intrusion response and investigation, and prosecution of computer terrorists.

Most of the money goes to funding government services. This may call into question government's commitment to shared cooperation with the public sector when most CIP money is spent within government on government infrastructure.

Of the funding for federal infrastructure protection $740 million of the almost $1.7 billion requested is slated for "system protection." To date the drafted report has not further defined what constitutes "system protection" in detail. Roughly half of the money requested for system protection has been for "multiple program areas" which are also not defined in the draft. Intrusion monitoring and response and threat, vulnerability and risk assessments have received the next greatest amount of requested funding as indicated by the $249.27 million and $229.15 million request in FY2001. The over-trends in CIP funding are shown in Tables 4.3 and 4.4, and Charts 4.1 and 4.2.

EFFORTS BY FEDERAL AGENCIES

Table 4.5 shows an OMB analysis of the major CIP activities in each federal department and agency. In shaping these activities, the federal government has attempted to coordinate the response of each agencies' own infrastructure security and to educate and partner with private industry. The role of each agency is matched up with national infrastructure sectors to which its mission relates, and each agency is given a responsibility to work with the private sector of that particular infrastructure.

Table 4.3
Government-wide Spending for Critical Infrastructure Protection (Current $US Millions)

	FY1998	FY1999	FY2000	FY2001
Federal Government				
Critical Infrastructure Protection	1,142.00	1,428.57	1,759.42	2,027.25
Federal Infrastructure Protection	1,038.79	1,278.91	1,584.26	1,699.03
Education and Training	37.54	48.50	79.45	105.00
Intrusion Monitoring and Response	127.63	186.27	213.37	249.27
Legislative Initiatives and Legal Issues	0.12	0.20	0.20	0.23
Multiple Program Areas	242.45	282.72	397.21	369.05
Reconstitution	26.19	30.18	16.29	5.64
System Protection	533.32	631.13	710.23	740.69
Threat/Vulnerability/Risk Assessments	71.56	99.92	167.51	229.15
CIP Assistance/Outreach to Private Sector	103.21	149.66	175.16	328.22
Education and Training	1.14	1.60	1.60	2.50
Intrusion Monitoring and Response	3.75	5.20	4.70	6.62
Legislative Initiatives and Legal Issues	1.58	2.60	2.60	3.60
Multiple Program Areas	37.99	70.78	61.14	133.92
Public Awareness/Outreach	0.00	0.00	2.30	3.10
Reconstitution	0.00	0.00	0.00	2.13
System Protection	37.31	43.15	57.05	72.14
Threat/Vulnerability/Risk Assessments	21.44	26.33	45.78	104.14

Table 4.4
Federal Spending on CIP by Agency: FY1998–FY2001 (Current $US Millions)

	FY1998	FY1999	FY2000	FY2001
Agriculture	0.70	1.22	2.51	17.89
Commerce	9.35	21.81	17.75	92.10
Education	3.59	4.45	5.23	2.51
Energy	1.50	3.60	21.98	45.30
EPA	0.12	0.24	0.08	2.30
FEMA	0.00	0.00	0.80	1.47
GSA	89.60	136.50	92.80	132.36
HHS	21.85	14.39	22.11	27.60
Interior	1.29	1.60	2.65	1.83
Justice	25.61	54.09	44.02	45.51
NASA	41.00	43.00	66.00	61.00
NSF	19.15	21.42	26.65	43.85
National Security	974.56	1185.22	1402.94	1458.91
NRC	0.00	0.20	0.00	0.25
OPM	0.00	0.00	2.00	7.00
Transportation	20.33	24.88	50.68	99.34
Treasury	22.91	48.89	76.21	87.03
Veterans Affairs	0.00	0.00	17.33	17.39

Source: Adapted by Anthony H. Cordesman.

For example, the Department of Commerce is the lead agency in the communications sector. The Department of Transportation is the lead agency for transportation CIP. The Treasury Department is the lead agency for banking and finance. DOE partners with the energy community, EPA provides a limited partnership with the water suppliers (which now fall mostly within state jurisdiction). DOJ/FBI is the lead agency for assistance to the law enforcement and emergency management community.

Department of Agriculture

Money slated for DOA federal infrastructure protection has grown from zero funding, across the board for any CIP related programs in FY1998.[63] In FY2001 DOA requested roughly $17.89 million for

Chart 4.1
Federal Spending on CIP by Activity: FY1998–FY2001 (Current $US Millions)

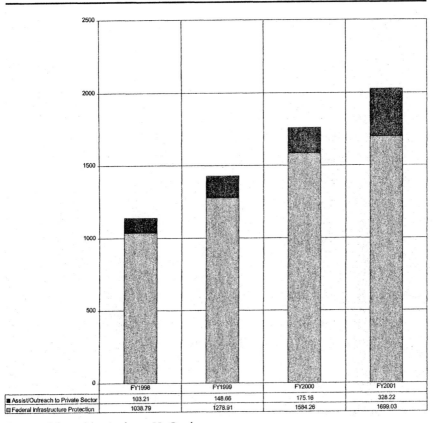

	FY1998	FY1999	FY2000	FY2001
■ Assist/Outreach to Private Sector	103.21	148.66	175.16	328.22
▨ Federal Infrastructure Protection	1038.79	1278.91	1584.26	1699.03

Source: Adapted by Anthony H. Cordesman.

protection of federal infrastructure and assistance/outreach to private sector a request raise of over $15 million from FY2000 and over a $16 million raise from FY1999.[64] Of the nearly $18 million dollar request, $16.89 million is to fund the protection of federal infrastructure side of CIP with the majority of the money going to system protection and intrusion monitoring and response. The rest of the money is earmarked for threat and vulnerability assessment. For public–private partnership the administration has requested $1 million, for threat vulnerability and assessments, funding has stayed between the $700,000 dollar range in FY1998 up to $1.4 million in FY2000.

Chart 4.2
Federal Spending on CIP by Agency: FY1998–FY2001 (Current $US Millions)

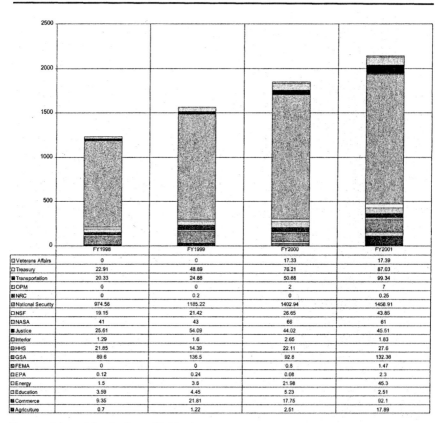

	FY1998	FY1999	FY2000	FY2001
▯ Veterans Affairs	0	0	17.33	17.39
▯ Treasury	22.91	48.89	76.21	87.03
▮ Transportation	20.33	24.88	50.68	99.34
▯ OPM	0	0	2	7
▮ NRC	0	0.2	0	0.25
▯ National Security	974.58	1185.22	1402.94	1458.91
▯ NSF	19.15	21.42	26.65	43.85
▯ NASA	41	43	66	61
▮ Justice	25.61	54.09	44.02	45.51
▯ Interior	1.29	1.6	2.65	1.83
▯ HHS	21.85	14.39	22.11	27.6
▯ GSA	89.6	136.5	92.8	132.36
▯ FEMA	0	0	0.8	1.47
▯ EPA	0.12	0.24	0.08	2.3
▯ Energy	1.5	3.8	21.98	45.3
▯ Education	3.59	4.45	5.23	2.51
▮ Commerce	9.35	21.81	17.75	92.1
▮ Agriculture	0.7	1.22	2.51	17.89

Source: Adapted by Anthony H. Cordesman.

Department of Commerce

The Department of Commerce (DOC) plays a lead role "in establishing and enhancing the partnership between the federal government and the private sector to protect the nation's infrastructure." As a result of PDD-63, the DOC was assigned three major functions: "the Critical Infrastructure Assurance Office (CIAO), lead agency responsibilities for the information and communications sector, and CIP research and development responsibilities."[65]

The bureaus within the department that support these activities are: the Bureau of Export Administration that houses CIAO. The National

Telecommunications and Information Agency (NTIA) which leads outreach and assistance to the information and communications sector. The National Institute of Standards and Technology (NIST), along with the National Oceanic and Atmospheric Administration and NTIA, conduct research to develop CIP technology, standards, and best practices. The following is a breakdown of the key DOC initiatives with FY2001 budget request, as reported by the "Annual Report to Congress on Combating Terrorism" 2000:

- **Lead Agency for Information and Communications Sector ($3.5million):** NTIA's responsibility as lead agency is to develop an effective partnership relationship with the private sector to identify and resolve infrastructure protection problems and technology needs. NTIA will raise industry awareness of the nature of threats and vulnerabilities within this sector and facilitate industry efforts in sharing information to improve preparedness against threats.
- **Critical Infrastructure Assurance Office ($6 million):** The CIAO functions as the Federal Government's interagency coordination mechanism for implementation of PDD-63. It supports the National Coordinator's work with government agencies in the private sector in developing a plan to reduce the exposure to attack of the Nation's critical infrastructures. It coordinates the Administration's Partnership for Critical Infrastructure Security, a public-private initiative designed to promote cross-industry dialogue and participation in developing the next version of the National Infrastructure Assurance Plan. Analytical support for the CICG and lead agencies includes assisting agencies in identifying their dependencies on critical infrastructures; summarizing key infrastructure laws; identifying and compiling cyber and physical security standards; cataloging training programs; and analyzing model mutual aid agreements to assist state and local governments and the private sector in protection and restoring critical facilities.
- **Institute for Information Infrastructure Protection (I3P) ($50 million):** The budget proposes the establishment of an Institute housed at NIST to work collaboratively with industry and academia on key information infrastructure protection technologies, filling research and other key technology gaps that neither the private sector nor the government's national security community would otherwise address. Research work will be performed at existing institutions including private corporations, universities, and nonprofit research institutes, seeking to engage the nation's finest technical experts to address priority research areas.
- **Expert Review Team ($5 million):** The budget proposes the establishment of a technical assistance team housed at NIST to assist agencies in adhering to Federal computer security requirements. The team would be responsible for helping Agencies identify vulnerabilities, plan secure systems, and

Table 4.5
Agency Spending for Critical Infrastructure Protection

	FY1998	FY1999	FY2000	FY2001
Department of Agriculture				
Critical Infrastructure Protection	0.70	1.22	2.51	17.89
Federal Infrastructure Protection	0.00	0.22	1.11	16.89
Intrusion Monitoring and Response	0.00	0.22	1.11	6.44
System Protection	0.00	0.00	0.00	9.00
Threat/Vulnerability/Risk Assessments	0.00	0.00	0.00	1.46
CIP Assistance/Outreach to Private Sector	0.70	1.00	1.40	1.00
Threat/Vulnerability/Risk Assessments	0.70	1.00	1.40	1.00
Department of Commerce				
Critical Infrastructure Protection	9.35	21.81	17.75	92.10
Federal Infrastructure Protection	2.00	10.84	6.75	15.58
Multiple Program Areas	0.00	3.00	1.50	3.00
System Protection	2.00	7.84	5.25	6.33
Threat/Vulnerability/Risk Assessments	0.00	0.00	0.00	6.25
CIP Assistance/Outreach to Private Sector	7.35	10.97	11.00	76.52
Education and Training	0.00	0.00	0.00	0.50
Intrusion Monitoring and Response	0.50	0.62	0.65	0.62
Multiple Program Areas	0.00	3.00	1.50	56.50
Public Awareness/Outreach	0.00	0.00	0.00	0.50
System Protection	6.85	7.35	7.85	9.85
Threat/Vulnerability/Risk Assessments	0.00	0.00	1.00	8.55

Department of Education

Critical Infrastructure Protection	2.51	5.23	4.45	3.59
Federal Infrastructure Protection	2.50	5.22	4.44	3.58
Education and Training	0.03	0.03	0.07	0.01
Intrusion Monitoring and Response	2.25	2.44	2.06	1.46
Reconstitution	0.00	0.52	0.51	0.39
System Protection	0.10	2.06	1.64	1.39
Threat/Vulnerability/Risk Assessments	0.13	0.17	0.16	0.33
CIP Assistance/Outreach to Private Sector	0.01	0.01	0.01	0.01
Multiple Program Areas	0.01	0.01	0.01	0.01

Department of Energy

Critical Infrastructure Protection	45.30	21.98	3.60	1.50
Federal Infrastructure Protection	32.30	17.56	1.80	0.00
Education and Training	3.50	1.00	1.00	0.00
Intrusion Monitoring and Response	9.30	7.34	0.80	0.00
Multiple Program Areas	2.00	1.00	0.00	0.00
System Protection	15.50	6.18	0.00	0.00
Threat/Vulnerability/Risk Assessments	2.00	2.04	0.00	0.00
CIP Assistance/Outreach to Private Sector	13.00	4.42	1.80	1.50
Intrusion Monitoring and Response	0.60	0.16	0.10	0.00
Legislative Initiatives and Legal Issues	0.60	0.00	0.00	0.00
Multiple Program Areas	1.50	0.80	1.50	1.50
Public Awareness/Outreach	0.20	2.00	0.00	0.00
Reconstitution	2.00	0.00	0.00	0.00
System Protection	1.70	0.00	0.00	0.00
Threat/Vulnerability/Risk Assessments	6.40	1.46	0.20	0.00

(continued)

Table 4.5 (continued)

	FY1998	FY1999	FY2000	FY2001
Environmental Protection Agency				
Critical Infrastructure Protection	**0.12**	**0.24**	**0.08**	**2.30**
Federal Infrastructure Protection	0.11	0.23	0.00	0.00
Threat/Vulnerability/Risk Assessment	0.11	0.23	0.00	0.00
Federal Emergency Management Agency				
Critical Infrastructure Protection	**0.00**	**0.00**	**0.80**	**1.47**
Federal Infrastructure Protection	0.00	0.00	0.00	1.17
Threat/Vulnerability/Risk Assessments	0.00	0.00	0.00	1.17
CIP Assistance/Outreach to Private Sector	0.00	0.00	0.80	0.30
Multiple Program Areas	0.00	0.00	0.80	0.15
Public Awareness/Outreach	0.00	0.00	0.00	0.15
General Services Administration				
Critical Infrastructure Protection	**0.00**	**3.00**	**0.00**	**15.40**
Federal Infrastructure Protection	0.00	2.00	0.00	15.40
Intrusion Monitoring and Response	0.00	2.00	0.00	15.40
CIP Assistance/Outreach to Private Sector	0.00	1.00	0.00	0.00
Multiple Program Areas	0.00	1.00	0.00	0.00
Department of Health and Human Services				
Critical Infrastructure Protection	**21.85**	**14.39**	**22.11**	**27.60**
Federal Infrastructure Protection	21.85	14.39	22.11	25.60
Multiple Program Areas	18.40	8.17	8.70	9.70

System Protection	2.45	5.02	12.21	14.70
Threat/Vulnerability/Risk Assessments	1.00	1.20	1.20	1.20
CIP Assistance/Outreach to Private Sector	0.00	0.00	0.00	2.00
Multiple Program Areas	0.00	0.00	0.00	2.00
Department of the Interior				
Critical Infrastructure Protection	1.29	1.60	2.65	1.83
Federal Infrastructure Protection	0.64	0.80	1.33	0.91
Threat/Vulnerability/Risk Assessments	0.64	0.80	1.33	0.91
CIP Assistance/Outreach to Private Sector	0.64	0.80	1.33	0.91
Department of Justice				
Critical Infrastructure Protection	25.61	54.09	44.02	45.51
Federal Infrastructure Protection	0.84	1.73	1.43	1.50
Legislative Initiatives and Legal Issues	0.12	0.20	0.20	0.23
Multiple Program Areas	0.72	1.54	1.24	1.27
CIP Assistance/Outreach to Private Sector	24.77	52.36	42.59	44.01
Legislative Initiatives and Legal Issues	1.58	2.60	2.60	3.07
Multiple Program Areas	23.19	49.76	39.98	40.94
National Aeronautics and Space Administration				
Critical Infrastructure Protection	41.00	43.00	66.00	61.00
Federal Infrastructure Protection	41.00	43.00	66.00	61.00
Education and Training	1.00	1.00	2.00	2.00
Intrusion Monitoring and Response	16.00	17.00	25.00	24.00
Multiple Program Areas	5.00	5.00	5.00	5.00
System Protection	18.00	19.00	32.00	28.00
Threat/Vulnerability/Risk Assessment	1.00	1.00	2.00	2.00

(continued)

Table 4.5 (continued)

	FY1998	FY1999	FY2000	FY2001
National Science Foundation				
Critical Infrastructure Protection	**19.15**	**21.42**	**26.65**	**43.85**
Federal Infrastructure Protection	0.57	0.60	0.63	10.87
Education and Training	0.00	0.00	0.00	10.20
System Protection	0.57	0.60	0.63	0.67
CIP Assistance/Outreach to Private Sector	18.58	20.82	26.02	32.98
Intrusion Monitoring and Response	0.00	0.51	0.53	0.54
Multiple Program Areas	0.00	0.00	-	4.00
System Protection	17.21	18.34	23.11	25.81
Threat/Vulnerability/Risk Assessments	1.37	1.97	2.38	2.63
National Security				
Critical Infrastructure Protection	**974.56**	**1,185.22**	**1,402.94**	**1,458.91**
Federal Infrastructure Protection	956.27	1,160.80	1,379.56	1,420.05
Education and Training	36.53	46.42	73.61	81.46
Intrusion Monitoring and Response	108.66	158.70	172.79	187.18
Multiple Program Areas	218.33	265.01	379.77	348.08
Reconstitution	25.50	29.17	15.40	5.19
System Protection	503.58	584.28	630.23	638.12
Threat/Vulnerability/Risk Assessment	63.67	77.22	107.75	160.01
CIP Assistance/Outreach to Private Sector	18.29	24.42	23.38	38.86
Intrusion Monitoring and Response	0.00	0.80	0.24	0.24
Multiple Program Areas	13.29	15.52	18.04	18.82
System Protection	5.00	7.15	5.10	4.80
Threat/Vulnerability/Risk Assessment	0.00	0.95	0.00	15.00

Nuclear Regulatory Commission				
Critical Infrastructure Protection	**0.25**	0.00	**0.20**	0.00
Federal Infrastructure Protection	0.25	0.00	0.20	0.00
Reconstitution	0.00	0.00	0.20	0.00
Threat/Vulnerability/Risk Assessment	0.25	0.00	0.00	0.00
Office of Personnel Management				
Critical Infrastructure Program	7.00	2.00	0.00	0.00
Federal Infrastructure Program	**7.00**	**2.00**	**0.00**	0.00
Education and Training	7.00	2.00	0.00	0.00
	7.00	2.00	0.00	0.00
Department of Transportation				
Critical Infrastructure Protection	**99.34**	50.68	**24.88**	20.33
Federal Infrastructure Protection	2.32	1.49	1.42	0.94
Reconstitution	0.45	0.37	0.30	0.30
System Protection	1.12	1.12	1.12	0.64
Threat/Vulnerability/Risk Assessments	0.75	0.00	0.00	0.00
CIP Assistance/Outreach to Private Sector	97.03	49.19	23.46	19.39
Intrusion Monitoring and Response	1.50	0.00	0.00	0.00
Multiple Program Areas	4.00	0.00	0.00	0.00
Public Awareness/Outreach	2.05	0.10	0.00	0.00
Reconstitution	0.13	0.00	0.00	0.00
System Protection	28.90	19.76	8.95	7.47
Threat/Vulnerability/Risk Assessments	60.45	29.33	14.51	11.92
Department of Treasury				
Critical Infrastructure Protection	**87.03**	76.21	**48.89**	22.91
Federal Infrastructure Protection	67.73	61.27	35.86	10.94
Intrusion Monitoring and Response	4.70	4.70	5.50	1.50
System Protection	10.93	4.47	11.06	4.64
Threat/Vulnerability/Risk Assessments	52.10	52.10	19.30	4.80

(continued)

Table 4.5 (continued)

	FY1998	FY1999	FY2000	FY2001
CIP Assistance/Outreach to Private Sector	11.96	13.03	14.96	19.30
Education and Training	1.14	1.60	1.60	2.00
Intrusion Monitoring and Response	3.25	3.17	3.12	3.12
Multiple Program Areas	0.00	0.00	0.00	4.00
Public Awareness/Outreach	0.00	0.00	0.20	0.20
System Protection	0.78	1.36	1.24	1.08
Threat/Vulnerability/Risk Assessments	6.80	6.90	8.80	8.90
Department of Veterans Affairs				
Critical Infrastructure Protection	0.00	0.00	17.33	17.39
Federal Infrastructure Protection	0.00	0.00	17.33	17.39
Education and Training	0.00	0.00	0.82	0.81
System Protection	0.00	0.00	15.60	15.65
Threat/Vulnerability/Risk Assessments	0.00	0.00	0.91	0.93

Source: Adapted by Steve Chu and Preston Golson from Executive Office of the President, Office Management and Budget, "Annual Report to Congress on Combating Terrorism." Figures part of the 2001 budget.

implement Critical Infrastructure Protection plans. The team would also assist agencies with specific computer security projects, including computer intrusion drills and security fixes for systems identified to have unacceptable security risks.

- **CIP Research and Development (13.3 million):** DOC's extensive research addresses deficiencies in current software development and assurance methods, including technology development for system survivability, secure Internet protocols, and encryption.[66]

Despite its seeming importance to CIP, DOC suffered a cut of $4 million from $21.8 million in FY99 enacted to $17.8 million in FY00 enacted.[67] Yet the Administration in FY01 is requesting a significant increase to $92.1 million giving the DOC the highest requested budget for CIP behind national security if enacted.

DOC status as a lead agency for CIP has not kept it from suffering budget cuts. Agency funding for federal infrastructure protection and assistance/outreach efforts was cut from $21.81 million in FY1999 to $17.75 million in FY2000. According to the report Congress rejected all of commerce's request for lead agency activities which accounted for $3.5 million.[68]

In FY2001, however, the administration has requested a considerable increase in funding to $92.10 million in the 01 budget. The cause for the significant rise in request lies in the DOC's fulfilling of its assigned PDD-63 functions. Of the $92.10 million, $3.5 million is to be allocated in the budget to allow DOC to serve as the lead agency for the information and communications sector. Six million dollars is to be assigned to CIAO. A great portion of the newly requested funds, $50 million, if enacted would go to the establishment of the Institute for Information Infrastructure Protection (I3P).

This new entity would be housed at NIST and tasked with the work of collaborating with industry and academia "on key information infrastructure protection technologies, filing research and other key technology gaps that neither the private sector nor the government's national security community would otherwise address. Research work will be performed at existing institutions including private corporations, universities, and non-profit research institutes, engaging our nation's finest technical experts to address priority research areas."[69]

Another $5 million would be used to establish an expert review team housed in NIST that would assist agencies in becoming compliant with federal computer security requirements. This team would help agencies identify vulnerabilities, plan secure systems, implement CIP plans, and assist with computer security projects such as computer intrusion drills and security fixes for at risk systems.[70]

A total of $13.3 million of the President's budget is to be marked for CIP R&D which, according to the report, includes "DOC's extensive research address deficiencies in current software development and assurance methods, including technology development for system survivability, secure Internet protocols, and encryption."[71] This prose raises some basic questions: Can $13 million of government funds really make a difference when private industry can kick in more in R&D?

Critical Infrastructure Assurance Office

Originally called the National Plan Coordination Staff in PDD-63, the Critical Infrastructure Assurance Office (CIAO) serves to coordinate several elements of the administration's CIP mechanisms.

Department of Energy

Being the lead agency for energy infrastructures, DOE's CIP responsibilities include collaborating with private sector energy infrastructure elements for critical infrastructure assurance.

Funding for CIP within DOE has grown from virtually nothing in FY1998, with an enacted budget of $1.5 million to a much larger requested budget of $45.3 million in FY2001. The greatest expansion of funds has been seen in the past two years. For FY1998 and FY1999 the department delegated little if any funds to CIP. For protection of federal infrastructure, DOE received no funds in FY1998 and $1.8 million in FY1999. In the past two fiscal years DOE has seen an increase in funding for federal infrastructure protection to $17.56 million in FY2000 and a requested $32.3 million in FY2001. The bulk of the money requested in FY2001 is set to go to system protection efforts with $15.5 million devoted to that effort in the report.

CIP outreach funding has increased from $1.5 million in FY1998 to $13 million requested in the FY2001 budget. Most of the funding requested in FY2001 is to go to threat, vulnerability, and risk assessments.

The programs highlighted by OMB in the report were the DOE CIP program and the Cyber Security Program. The DOE CIP program is for the focus on "thrust areas of Analysis and Risk Management and Protection and Mitigation Technologies." The report states that this will provide real-time control mechanisms, integrated multi-sensor and warning systems, and risk management and consequence analysis tools that will help the national energy sector address the physical and cyber-threats to, and vulnerabilities of the energy infrastructures. DOE will develop infrastructure interdependence tools to improve the capability to assess the technical, economic and national security implications of cascading energy infrastructure disruptions and to improve the reliability and security of the Nation's interdependent energy grid. This program will involve collaboration between DOE and the major stakeholders, including private sector owners of energy elements, other federal agencies involved in critical infrastructure protection, and state and local governments. The national laboratories, academia, and private research organizations will participate in developing and implementing the research program.[72]

A total of $30 million is requested for the Cyber Security Program to allow DOE to fulfill its responsibilities in protecting its cyber-systems. This program supports development of high level, consistent, risk management-based policies and implementation guidance for the protection of cyber-assets; training to provide consistent core training requirements for cyber-security professionals, system administrators, senior management, and general users; operations to provide departmental capabilities for cyber-incident response, core cyber-security architecture, cyber-intrusion detection and reporting, and public key infrastructure architecture; and technical development to provide tools to eliminate cyber-security vulnerabilities where commercial or government products are not available.[73]

As indicated by the recent rise in funding for CIP within the DOE, however, DOE is just beginning to get the kind of funding needed for CIP preparedness. DOE only devoted limited funding to protection of its infrastructure in 1998 and only $1.8 million in 1999.

Environmental Protection Agency and GAO Audits

The balance of EPA spending for CIP is requested for protection of the water sector from the threat of terrorist attack.[74] An October 1999 agency review showed that the EPA had several security weaknesses in its computer operating systems and agency-wide network. These systems and network support most of the EPA's mission-related and financial operations. GAO also noted that EPA's own records cited several serious computer incidents in the last two years.[75]

Health and Human Services

Unlike DOE, HHS received significant funding in FY1998 of $21.85 million. HHS has seen these funds drop in FY1999 to $14.39 million, rise back up to $22.11 million in FY2000, and see a request of $27.60 million in FY2001.[76] The OMB report is not clear on what this funding is used for, only that the vast majority of funds are aimed at the protection of federal infrastructure (the total balance of the funds were devoted to this area in FY98, FY99, and FY00). Most of the funds within this total were spent on multiple program areas in FY98 and FY99 and then on systems protection in the following two fiscal years.[77] OMB highlighted no special programs for HHS.

Department of Interior

Neither the OMD nor DOE provide a detailed analysis of the department's spending on critical infrastructure protection.

Department of Justice

With the FBI being the lead federal agency for coordinating emergency law enforcement services in responding to critical infrastructure attacks, DOJ requested in the president's budget $45.51 million for CIP.[78] Very little of the funding for the past four fiscal years has gone to protection of federal infrastructures—only $1.5 million in FY2001.[79]

The majority of the funds are allocated for public assistance. OMB reporting places this spending in the somewhat nebulous category of multiple programs. However, when looking at the highlighted program list it is apparent that the majority of the money will be placed in the National Infrastructure Protection Center ($20 million) and computer intrusion squads ($22 million).[80]

NASA

NASA has consistently received funding for protection of its infrastructure. This funding has consistently been spent within the department on intrusion monitoring and response ($16 million in FY98, $17 million in FY99, $25 million in FY00, and $24 million in FY01) and system protection ($18 million in FY98, $19 million in FY99 and $32 and $28 million in FY00 and FY01 requested).[81]

GAO Assessments of NASA Information Security

In a May 1999 report, GAO declared that tests done on 10 field sites had found that some of NASA's mission critical systems were vulnerable to penetration. While all systems GAO testers gained access had effective security measures to deny further access, some systems could be compromised to the point that an intruder could have "disrupted NASA's ongoing command and control operations and stolen, modified, or destroyed system software and data."[82] GAO linked these weaknesses to what GAO deduced as NASA's inability to effectively and consistently manage IT security throughout the agency. GAO reported that NASA:[83]

- did not effectively assess risks or evaluate needs. One hundred thirty-five of the 155 mission-critical systems that we reviewed did not meet all of NASA's requirements for risk assessments.
- did not effectively implement policies and controls. NASA's guidance did not specify what information can be posted on public World Wide Web sites or how mission-critical systems should be protected from well-known Internet threats.
- was not monitoring policy compliance or the effectiveness of controls. NASA had not conducted an agency-wide review of IT security at its 10 field centers since 1991. Furthermore, the security of 60 percent of the systems that we reviewed had not been independently audited.
- was not providing required computer security training. NASA had no structured security training curriculum.
- did not centrally coordinate responses to security incidents. NASA field centers were not reporting incidents to the NASA Automated Systems Incident Response Capability (NASIRC).

GAO recommended a five-category approach to dealing with NASA's information security weaknesses.[84]

We are recommending that the NASA administrator implement an effective agency-wide security program that includes improvements in five categories: assessing risks and evaluating needs, implementing policies and controls, monitoring compliance with policy and effectiveness of controls, providing computer security training, and coordinating responses to security incidents. NASA concurs in all of our recommendations.

In detail GAO recommended that[85]

- Assessing risks and evaluating needs, which includes the following:
- Developing and instituting a review process to ensure that managers conduct complete risk assessments for all major systems prior to the systems becoming operational, upon significant change, or at least every 3 years.
- Formally authorizing all systems before they become operational and at least every three years
- Implementing policies and controls, which includes the following
- Streamlining the policy-making and standards-setting process for IT security so that guidance can be issued and modified promptly to address changes in threats and vulnerabilities introduced by rapidly evolving computer and telecommunication technologies.

- Developing and issuing guidance that specifies information that is appropriate for posting on World Wide Web sites and distinguishes this from information that is sensitive and should be more closely controlled.
- Developing and issuing guidance that identifies systems, including those involved in the command and control of orbiting spacecraft that require strong user authentication.
- Monitoring compliance with policy and effectiveness of controls, which includes the following:
- Developing and implementing a management oversight process to periodically monitor and enforce field centers' compliance with agency-wide policy.
- Ensuring that independent audits or reviews of systems' security controls are performed at least every 3 years and that identified weaknesses are expeditiously corrected.
- Providing required computer security training, which includes the following:
- Developing and implementing a structured program for ensuring that NASA employees receive periodic training in computer security to provide them with awareness, knowledge, and skills necessary to protect sensitive information and mission critical systems.
- Modifying relevant contracts to include provisions for ensuring that NASA contract personnel are similarly trained.
- Developing and implementing a program for certifying that NASA civil servants and contract employees are competent to discharge their IT security-related responsibilities
- Coordinating responses to security incidents, which includes the following:
- Clarifying policy and procedures for mandatory reporting of security incidents to NASIRC.
- Strengthening the role of NASIRC in disseminating vulnerability information within NASA, analyzing threats in real time and developing effective countermeasures for ongoing attacks.
- We also recommend that the NASA CIO review the specific vulnerabilities and suggested actions provided to field center officials at the conclusion of our penetration testing, determine and implement appropriate security countermeasures, and track the implementation and/or disposition of these actions.

NATIONAL SCIENCE FOUNDATION

NSF plays a role in protecting federal infrastructure through education and training ($10.2 million for FY2001) and assistance to the public sector through system protection ($32.98 million).[86] Most of the $32 million for public sector assistance is most likely going to research and development, as indicated by the OMB report.

OMB also reports that NSF will provide support for research in FY2001 in areas including networking, high performance computing, and software that will enable computer and communications systems to be safer, more reliable, and free from intrusions. NSF will also provide support for research in critical infrastructure protection by sponsoring work on software development methods to improve the predictability and security of critical software systems, innovative approaches to fault tolerance, and modeling, simulation, and optimization of control of electric power systems.[87]

NATIONAL SECURITY COMMUNITY

The national security community dominates the budget regarding CIP. In the community DoD is considered the lead agency for protecting critical defense infrastructures against attack and ensuring the integrity and security of DoD information systems.[88]

The OMB report omits any data on U.S. offensive and retaliatory cyber- and information warfare capability and provides few details on the allocation of over $1.458 billion requested in FY2001, which is more than half of the entire CIP budget. What can be understood from the OMB report is that nearly all of that money is spent on the protection of federal infrastructure ($1.42 billion). Of that $1.42 billion, almost half goes to system protection ($638.12 million) and over $300 million is requested for multiple programs. Over $100 million is spent in both intrusion monitoring and response, and threat, vulnerability, and risk assessments with $187.18 million and $160 million respectively.

A total of $460 million of the highlighted programs is delegated for R&D purposes. A total of $177 million is to be spent on public key infrastructures. Fourteen million dollars will be used for developing computer network defense capability. OMB mentions funding for operation and maintenance which will pay over 2,800 civilians involved in information assurance and support activities. OMB does not mention a cost for that particular program.

It should be noted, however, that all of these figures fail to address the scale of offensive information warfare and cyber-attack capabilities within the national security community. They focus almost solely on defense efforts, and this approach to programming and budgeting reinforces the massive disconnect between cyber-offense and cyber-defense that characterizes all of the public literature on critical infrastructure protection.

This highlights the problem of focusing largely on defense in most federal critical infrastructure protection planning, rather than deterrence and active offensive response. It can be argued that such a focus is proper in dealing with low to moderate level attacks and threats because of the difficulty of attribution and the limits to the technology available for retaliation and counterattack. However, it is striking that no public federal assessment of these trade-offs seems to be available, and that the national security community has failed to address them in ways which can guide other elements of government and the private sector.

These problems are reinforced by the lack of any apparent net technical assessment effort to assess the balance between offense and defense, and vulnerability. There does not seem to be anything approaching an adequate and integrated analytic underpinning for programming the critical infrastructure protection efforts of the national security community, and this inevitably means that other federal agencies, state and local governments, businesses, NGOs, and utilities also lack proper priorities and guidance.

The Role of the Department of Defense

The Department of Defense is a critical player in the nation's effort to conduct offensive information and cyber-warfare, and its ability to deter or respond to foreign attacks. Virtually no data are public on this aspect of its capabilities, although—as has been discussed earlier—the department does have operational plans to carry out such attacks and is known to have developed detailed contingency plans for Desert Storm, Desert Fox, and NATO's intervention in Kosovo.

At the same time, few federal agencies are as dependent on secure information systems as the Department of Defense. The Defense Department has roughly 10,000 computer systems and 1.5 million individual computers. Arthur Money, the assistant secretary of defense for command, control, communications, and intelligence, told a House Armed Services subcommittee in March 2000 that about 2,000 of these systems are "mission-critical," and "must work for [the DoD] to successfully execute its myriad missions."

Over 95 percent of all DoD communications utilize the public switched network. This includes supporting such critical defense missions as the movement of troops and operational plans, procurement, and weapons systems maintenance. Secretary of Defense William Cohen's Annual Report to the President and the Congress for the year 2000 stated,

> DoD is committed to taking full advantage of opportunities provided by the information age's concepts and technologies in the 21st century. Cre-

ating and leveraging information superiority and exploiting the potential of Space are on DoD's critical path to the future. The synergy resulting from the consolidation of Information Superiority and Chief Information Officer (CIO) functions under the Assistant Secretary of Defense for Command, Control, Communications, and Intelligence (ASD(C3I)) continues to yield significant technical, operational, and financial benefits. The consolidation of space policy development and oversight and closer coordination with the Intelligence Community resulted in space concepts being better integrated into defense strategy and processes. These actions create and leverage information superiority.

The information age provides an opportunity to move from an approach to war preoccupied with uncertainty and damage control to one that leverages information to create competitive advantage. The United States currently enjoys a superior information position over potential adversaries by virtue of its ability to collect, process, protect, and distribute relevant and accurate information in a timely manner while denying this capability to adversaries.

This information edge is translated directly into increased effectiveness by enabling emerging network–centric concepts designed to leverage improved situation awareness. Thus, information superiority is reflected in the twin revolutions, the Revolutions in Military Affairs and Business Affairs. These twin revolutions are mutually supportive as improved business processes result in additional resources for combat capabilities increasing the tooth to tail ratio.

Information superiority is the critical enabler of the transformation of the department currently in progress. The results of research, analyses, and experiments designed to create and leverage information superiority, reinforced by recent experiences in Kosovo, are very encouraging. They demonstrate that the availability of information and the ability to share it results in enhanced mission effectiveness and improved efficiencies. This evidence points to increased speed of command, a higher tempo of operations, greater lethality, less fratricide and collateral damage, increased survivability, streamlined combat support, and more effective force synchronization.

The ability to move information quickly where it is needed and to create shared awareness provides an opportunity to develop new concepts of operation and approaches to command and control (C2) that are more responsive and provide greater flexibility. To achieve their full potential, these new concepts may require changes in organization, doctrine, material, and the like—changes that need to be co-evolved along with the development of new operational concepts and approaches to command and control. New approaches to command and control include integrating the now separate and sequential planning and execution processes to achieve greater agility and flexibility and the capability for self-synchronizing forces. Based upon a common understanding of the situation and the commander's intent, these forces are able to quickly respond in a coordinated fashion. Information superiority provides enhanced flexibility and agility, allowing U.S. forces to be more proactive and shape the battle-field.

Patterns of Attack and Response

The Department of Defense is a nearly constant target for attacks that range from random hacking to actions by states. Arthur Money, told a House Armed Services subcommittee in March 2000 that, "We are probed on a daily basis by those who are trying, or planning, to disrupt our nation's military capabilities . . . a few nation state operatives do major downloading of unclassified materials."[89]

Money testified that one "seminal event" that led the department to improve its computer security problems occurred in February 1998. Some youths in California, acting under the direction of an Israeli, took advantage of a "well-known vulnerability in Sun software" to break into the Solaris operating system used by defense agencies. The attacks came as preparations were underway for a possible military operation against Iraq. John J. Hamre, then Deputy Secretary of Defense, testified in 1999 that these attacks "were widespread, systematic and showed a pattern that indicated they might be the preparation for a coordinated attack on the defense information infrastructure." Military computer administrators had been warned about the weaknesses that the California hackers exploited, but many had failed to heed the warning and patch their systems.[90]

One important result, was that the department placed important limits on its ties to the Internet.[91] The Deputy Secretary of Defense issued a memo on September 24, 1998 that called for a department-wide effort to limit the information available on the Web, and to establish comprehensive risk management procedures to determine the value of placing data on the Web versus the security risk to the department and those serving in it. It called on the department to eliminate access to any data that might be used to gather information on operations, plans, troop movements, critical personnel information, and unit locations affecting operations. It also called for a C^{4}I architecture to protect sensitive, but unclassified information, plans to use reserve assets to strengthen the department's cyber-defenses, comprehensive training in cyber-security, and new procedures to ensure the review of software, data bases, and systems.

According to a department report issued in December 2000, the Defense Department suffered more than 22,000 electronic attacks on its computer systems in 1999 and about 14,000 in the first seven months of 2000. In 1999, the department detected 22,144 attempts to probe, scan, hack into, infect with viruses, or disable its computers. Roughly three percent (or more than 600) of those incidents caused temporary shutdowns or other damage. About one percent (or roughly 200) were intrusions by hackers who managed to break into unclassified computer systems. The number of attacks rose approximately 10 percent in the first seven months of 2000, and the percentage that have caused damage or resulted in intrusions is about the same.[92]

The department reported that the "vast majority of those attacks were either harmless or caused only petty harassment." It also indicated, however, that hackers believed to be working for foreign countries had broken into unclassified computer systems in a few cases, and downloaded large amounts of information. The department reported that no incidents were detected that were able to enter the Department of Defense's classified computer systems. These figures reported the departments first effort to make a really accurate count of the number of attacks because it only installed devices to monitor attempts by hackers to penetrate its computers at the end of 1998.[93]

Money predicted that the number of attacks was "going to increase in the future." He also indicated why designing less vulnerable systems may be at least as critical as improving defenses. He reported that a majority of the attacks that caused damage "come through vulnerabilities in existing software, most of it from commercial companies," such as Microsoft, Netscape, and Lotus. He stated that the department was "putting more and more effort into testing" off-the-shelf software and was working with major software companies in the design stages. Money stated, however, that "there is hardly any way to prevent" vulnerabilities from creeping into the millions of lines of commercial computer code. He noted that code is also written in India, Ireland, Israel, and other countries. "On a lot of these [programs], we don't know where the code is written." Other officials stated that most vulnerabilities were unintentional, but some seemed to be "trapdoors" deliberately left by the authors of the software to allow intrusions, while others were "backdoors" that were designed to help systems administrators that had been "discovered by kids and hackers and used to harass the systems." A Pentagon official added, "we are not buying such off-the-shelf products in our most sensitive systems."

These attack patterns led Congress to allocate an additional $163 million for computer security into the fiscal 2001 defense appropriations bill. At the same time, the House-Senate conferees' report on the bill warned that the new funds "will be of limited value if the software used by the department has been designed with intentional weaknesses to permit future unauthorized access." The conference report directed the Pentagon "to carefully consider the origin of all software used in developing or upgrading information technology or national security systems."[94]

It is also clear that these effort present problems in terms of skilled manpower. The department announced in December 2000 that it planned to recruit hundreds of reserve component information technology specialists in coming years to fill positions in several new military "cyber-security" organizations to ensure that American war fighters could dominate military computer information warfare in future conflicts. Rudy de Leon, the Deputy Secretary of Defense stated that "information operations has emerged as an area that is extremely well-suited to integration of reserve capabilities. Members of the reserve and National Guard are often way ahead by the very nature of their civilian employment, trained in their workplaces to exploit technology."

The department reported that it needed 182 reserve component officers and enlisted members to man the five organizations for fiscal 2001 and 2002, officials said. Numbers of people in each organization will vary. The total number of people in the units is expected to grow to more than 600 through fiscal 2007. The reserve component technicians and their units were assigned to support the Defense Information Security Agency, Arlington, Virginia; the Joint Task Force–Computer Network Defense, Arlington; the National Security Agency, Fort Meade, Maryland; the Joint Information Operations Center, Kelly Air Force Base, Texas; and the Information Operations Technical Center, Fort Meade.[95]

The department reported that the need for DoD to safeguard its computerized information systems was highlighted by recent "cyber-warfare" between Israeli and Palestinian computer technicians featuring the defacing of opponents' Web sites and massive "jamming" of digital information conduits by email saturation and virus "mail." It also reported that the decision to upgrade DoD's information security infrastructure originated from a recommendation from the reserve component employment 2005 study, which suggested new ways to employ reserve forces as part of fostering improved integration in the total force. Reserve component members who work for info-tech industry firms like Microsoft and IBM were found to make good fits for the new organizations.

Major DoD Cyber-defense Programs

The Department of Defense has major programs designed to protect its information systems that are reinforced by the physical protection measures it has taken in response to the threat posed by other forms of terrorism:

> The Department of Defense, being the largest organization in the nation, faces significant information technology challenges in its efforts

to ensure the continuity of critical missions and systems in the face of Y2K-related problems. Over one-third of all mission critical computer systems in the federal government are within DoD. DoD treated the Year 2000 problem as if it were a cyber-attack directed at the very core of its military capability—at the ability to obtain, process, and control information. Securing systems for 2000 provided numerous lessons that will translate well to efforts in securing the critical information infrastructure in the future.

Y2K efforts have led to the best ever accounting of DoD systems and status. The information management structure now in place meets the requirements of the Clinger-Cohen Act. The enormous effort and awareness of IT generated by the Year 2000 problem has resulted in significant progress across the board in information superiority.

Information Assurance

Information Assurance, a critical component of DoD's operational readiness, ensures that the DII is capable of providing continuous and dependable service. IA depends on the continuous integration of personnel, operational, and technical capabilities to guarantee the availability, integrity, authenticity, confidentiality, and non-repudiation of information services, while providing the means to efficiently reconstitute these vital services following an attack.

In August 1998, DoD created the Joint Task Force–Computer Network Defense (JTF–CND), with a mission of coordinating and directing the defense of DoD computer systems and computer networks including the coordination of DoD defensive actions with non-DoD government agencies and appropriate private organizations. In June 1999, the JTF–CND reached its full operational capability. Effective October 1, 1999, the Commander in Chief, United States Space Command, was assigned the responsibility for Computer Network Defense (CND). Detailed studies are underway to identify core functions and develop an integrated, defense-wide, enterprise CND policy and assignment of responsibilities.

In May 1999, the Deputy Secretary of Defense issued the defense-wide PKI policy that requires the use of a common, integrated DoD PKI to enable security services at multiple levels of assurance, provides a solid foundation for IA capabilities across the department, and mandates an aggressive approach in acquiring and using a PKI that meets DoD requirements for all information assurance services.

Critical Infrastructure Protection

CIP addresses the protection of the critical assets and infrastructures DoD relies upon to accomplish its mission. A CIP Plan went into effect in January 1999 to ensure an integrated approach to CIP. The ASD(C3I) was designated the Department's Chief Infrastructure Assurance Officer (CIAO), and senior DoD executives have been designated as CIAOs for each infrastructure. The department began development of an analytic and assessment capability for the Defense infrastructures, leveraging existing capabilities that had been focused on commercial infrastructures. The ASD (C3I) has also been designated at the Functional Coordinator for National Defense, responsible (under Presidential Decision Directive 63) for coordinating all the CIP-related national defense activities of the U.S. government, ensuring that the comprehensive approach DoD is applying to its internal infrastructures is supported nationally and internationally by the other federal departments and agencies as well as allies and coalition partners.

Security

DoD needs security policies and programs that pace the revolutionary changes in technology and combat on the modern battlefield. Policies must focus on providing protection based on assessments of threats and the danger and consequences of compromise for the most critical and vulnerable information, systems, capabilities, people, and facilities. The department requires an active security paradigm that includes the following steps:

- Establish Criticality. Identify what must be protected and determine the protection requirements, analyze what is required to accomplish the mission, assess protective and deterrence systems, determine vulnerabilities to the threat environment, establish a degree of assurance to determine acceptable risk.

- Prepare. Reduce the threat by establishing a high level of assurance in the trustworthiness and reliability of people, practices, systems, and programs.

- Protect Assets. Control asset sharing, isolating information and capabilities based on need-to-know; mitigate known operational deficiencies and vulnerabilities; employ a defense in-depth strategy; and employ new technology to enforce or support security policy.

- Detect. Actively seek potential isolated and correlated threats or problems, particularly that may result in future malicious or anomalous activity.

- Respond. React to isolated or correlated anomalous or malicious activity, fix technology-based problems and correct suspected and actual unacceptable behavior using sound personnel and security management practices, seek legal or other management remedies as appropriate and when necessary.

- Strengthen Foundation. Refine security policy constructs, programs, and practices to anticipate the changing threat environment; deconflict security requirements to foster information sharing while maintaining need-to-know; strengthen personnel management practices to provide a motivated, skilled, and security-responsive workforce; establish and maintain mission-related performance measures; develop standards of professional competence for security practitioners and enhance awareness and training to ensure information is tailored for the designated audience.

Developing and implementing a new vision of security in the information age requires recognition of the globalization of the defense industrial base and the closer integration of foreign countries in defense production. These trends will require changes in the existing security paradigm.

The department established a single office within the Office of the Secretary of Defense responsible for CI, Security, IA, CIP, and IO to ensure a coherent approach to these issues; established the Defense Information Assurance Program to better integrate the information assurance requirements and budgets of the DoD components, implemented a new certification process for systems administrators; and contributed personnel to the National Infrastructure Protection Center.

The department implemented the Information Assurance Vulnerability Alert process that disseminates information threat warning and remediation messages throughout DoD and monitors implementation of countermeasures, issued new guidance for Web pages to prevent inadvertent disclosure of sensitive information, and established a Joint Web Risk Assessment Cell to monitor compliance.

The Department of Defense is also developing offensive capabilities that can be used for deterrent and retaliatory purposes, although little unclassified data are available on these programs:

Information operations support the objectives of the National Security Strategy by enhancing information superiority and influencing foreign perceptions. The department's emerging concept for IO will be the basis for aligning strategy and policy across DoD. When approved, the strategic concept will guide and integrate IO policy, organization, and implementation and the research, development, and acquisition of IO capabilities.

To protect information, maintain information superiority, and improve preparedness, DoD is employing Red Teams, which are interdisciplinary, threat-based opposing forces to expose and exploit IO vulnerabilities of friendly forces. The department is preparing policy to standardize the methodology for conducting DoD Red Team operations.

The department is developing an IO resource baseline to identify DoD component IO-related efforts. This will provide the Department's leadership with great insight into DoD component IO resource, R&D efforts, and organizational focus, allowing greater resource efficiencies and DoD IO program integration.

Based on IO experience in support of Kosovo operations, DoD now has the makings of an IO framework from which to deal with future coalition/allied warfare issues to achieve/maintain information superiority. DoD education programs continue to be offered and are available to federal and military personnel. IO continues to be integrated into military exercises and wargames.

GAO Critiques of DoD Efforts: The 1996 Study

In a September 1996 GAO issued a report to the Secretary of Defense, the DISA director, and the CIOs of the military departments and other Defense agencies aimed at,[96]

- Empowering the DoD CIO to establish a comprehensive, department-wide information security program;
- Ensuring that security programs of the military departments and Defense agencies are consistent with the department program; and
- Periodically reporting on progress in improving controls over information security

The 1996 report listed ten recommendations, each of which DoD has reported to have taken corrective actions on. The recommendations for the 1996 report are as follows:[97]

I. We recommend that the Secretary of Defense assign clear responsibility and accountability within the Office of the Secretary of Defense, the military services, and the Defense agencies for ensuring the successful implementation of an information security program that includes, for example, department-wide policies for preventing, detecting, and responding to hacker attacks on Defense information systems.

II. We further recommend that you direct the DoD CIO to develop and implement a comprehensive DoD-wide computer security management program that includes the hacker prevention policies we previously recommended as well as

- establishing a risk-based control program to assess computer security in DoD computer systems,
- developing and implementing effective security policies and related control techniques, and
- reporting to DoD managers on security issues impacting their information processing systems.

III. We also recommend that you direct the Deputy Secretary of Defense to ensure that the duties established for the military departments' and Defense agencies' CIOs include reporting on ongoing computer security efforts and activities to the DoD CIO for review, assessment, and appropriate action to ensure proper coordination and an integrated information technology structure within the Department.

IV. Further, you should direct the DoD CIO to review and assess the specific deficiencies noted and establish a process to address them.

V. In addition, we recommend that the DISA Director, the CIOs of the military departments, and the CIOs of the other Defense agencies submit their policies and procedures to improve general computer controls to the DoD CIO for review, assessment, and appropriate action to ensure a comprehensive security approach is operational throughout the Department. Such policies and procedures should

- limit computer system access authorizations to only those who need access to perform their work responsibilities, and are periodically reviewed to ensure their continued need;

- require sensitive data files and critical production programs to be identified and successful and unsuccessful access to them to be monitored;

- strengthen security software standards in critical areas, such as by preventing the reuse of passwords and ensuring that security software is implemented and maintained in accordance with the standards;

- control physical security at computer facilities; and

- provide for completing and testing disaster recovery plans.

VI. To ensure that general computer controls are improved at the DMCs, we recommend that the DoD CIO direct the DISA Director to develop and implement a comprehensive computer security program at the DMCs, consistent with the DoD-wide program, that includes the elements outlined in this report. These elements encompass

- policies and procedures to ensure that access to DMC computer facilities is appropriately granted and periodically reviewed,

- clearly defined roles and responsibilities of DMC employees, information system security officers, and security managers, and

- security oversight at each DMC to monitor, measure, test, and report on the ongoing effectiveness of computer system, network, and process controls.

VII. In addition, we recommend that the CIOs of the military departments and the Defense agencies submit plans for coordinating with DISA to improve computer controls affecting DMC operations to the DoD CIO for review, assessment, and appropriate actions. Greater cooperation is necessary, for example, to

- determine who is given access to computer systems applications,

- identify critical computer systems applications to be covered by disaster recovery plans, and

- ensure that locally designed software application program changes are in accordance with prescribed policies and procedures.

VIII. Also, the DISA Director and the CIOs of the military departments and Defense agencies should provide their plans to the DoD CIO, for review, assessment, and appropriate action to ensure that computer system security reviews are performed as part of future transfers of computer systems to the DMCs.

IX. Further, the DoD CIO should monitor implementation of those plans.

X. Finally, to strengthen DoD's computer security program in a coordinated and timely manner, we recommend that you

- direct the DoD CIO to monitor and to periodically report on the status of the actions taken to improve computer security throughout DoD and

- ensure that the DoD CIO has the necessary authority to ensure that there are adequate computer security controls throughout DoD, including the military departments and Defense agencies.

The GAO's 1999 Recommendations

In the August 1999 report the GAO reaffirmed the recommendations of September 1996 and added additional recommendations to "realize the full potential and maximize the effectiveness of DISA's security oversight program, the DIAP, and other DoD IA initiatives . . ." GAO recommended that the Secretary of Defense[98]

- Direct the DISA Director to expand the Security Readiness Review process to include timely and independent verification of the corrective actions reported by DMCs or other responsible parties
- Direct the DoD CIO to ensure that the Defense-wide Information Assurance Program defines how its efforts will be coordinated with the Joint Task Force and other related initiatives.

The GAO noted an improvement in DISA's processes to identify information security weaknesses.[99]

Our reports identified pervasive information security weaknesses in DoD and made recommendations for correcting them. While some corrective actions had been initiated to address our recommendations, our current review found that weaknesses persisted in every area of general controls.

Among the DoD components evaluated, only DISA had begun to establish a comprehensive process to identify and resolve information security weaknesses. DISA was issuing technical guidance to establish minimum standards for configuring system software and was implementing systematic entity-wide inspections to monitor effectiveness of computer controls. As a result, DISA had identified and resolved thousands of control weaknesses.

The GAO report on DoD Information Security also found, however, that serious weaknesses created a continued risk to defense operations. The report cited that these weaknesses impaired DoD's:[100]

> ability to (1) control physical and electronic access to its systems and data, (2) ensure that software running on its systems is properly authorized, tested, and functioning as intended, (3) limit employees' ability to perform incompatible functions, and (4) resume operations in the event of a disaster. As a result, numerous Defense functions, including weapons and supercomputer research, logistics, finance, procurement, personnel management, military health, and payroll, have already been adversely affected by system attacks of fraud.

The GAO found that the DoD's massive information processing systems included over 2.1 million computers, over 10,000 local area networks, and over 100 long distance networks.[101] It listed the following weaknesses and recommendations for correcting them in its August 1999 report:[102]

> In our current review we found that significant DoD information security weaknesses in general computer controls persisted for all the components evaluated, including DISA. The following sections give examples illustrating the types of weaknesses we found in access controls, application software development and change controls, and segregation of duties, system software controls, and service continuity controls.
>
> Access controls limit or detect inappropriate access to computer data, programs, facilities, and equipment to protect these resources against unauthorized modification, disclosure, loss, or impairment. Access controls include physical protections, such as gates and guards, and logical controls, which are built into software to authenticate users (through passwords or other means) and to restrict their access to certain data, programs, transactions, or commands. DoD policy states that access to automated information systems should be restricted based on one's need-to-know.
>
> We found, however, that users were granted access to computer resources that exceeded what they required to carry out their job responsibilities, including sensitive system privileges for which they had no need. On one system, systems support personnel had the ability to change data in the system audit log. On three systems, we tested the accounts of 12 users having access to a command that would allow them to substitute

an unauthorized data file for a legitimate file. Seven out of 12 did not have a need to use this command. We also found user accounts that had certain privileges—including sensitive security administration privileges—for which no evidence of authorization was available. Access authorization was poorly documented or undocumented for users at every site; management estimated that on one system more than 20,000 users were not authorized in writing.

Periodic review of user access privileges and monitoring of security violations and the use of powerful commands, utilities, and changes to sensitive files and records (such as user access profiles) are essential to preventing and detecting unauthorized activity. However, we found at every location we visited that there was inadequate periodic review of user access privileges to ensure that those privileges continued to be appropriate. Also, while the logging of security violations and access to sensitive resources had improved, these audit logs were not being consistently reviewed. Similarly, we found that data processing customers were not updating users' access levels to reflect changes in their access requirements or to cancel the access of terminated employees.

Password management, though improved, was still weak in some areas. Users were not required to change their passwords often enough and in some cases were never required to change their passwords. Users were not prevented from using easily guessed passwords. These practices increase the risk that passwords will be guessed and systems will be compromised.

User accountability was also weakened by the use of generic (group) user accounts, wherein a single account is used by two or more users, contrary to DISA standards. In the case of one generic user account having system privileges, not only was the password known to multiple users, but it was neither encrypted in the system nor required to be changed periodically.

Application software development and change controls prevent unauthorized programs or modifications to programs from being implemented to ensure that the software functions as intended. Program change control policies and procedures include review and approval of application change requests, independent review and testing of program changes, documentation of program changes, and formal authorization to implement those changes, along with the access controls necessary to ensure that these objectives are met.

We found that structured methodologies for designing, developing, and maintaining applications were inadequate or nonexistent. There was no requirement for users to document the planning and review of application changes and to test them to ensure that the system functioned as intended. Also, application programs were not adequately documented with a full description of the purpose and function of each module, which increases the risk that a developer making program changes will unknowingly subvert new or existing application controls.

One fundamental technique of program change control is the use of two or more computer processing environments to segregate the test and development versions of application programs and data from the production resources (those versions approved and currently being used by the data processing customer). We found that application programmers, users, and computer operators had direct access to production resources, increasing the risk that unauthorized changes to production programs and data could be made and not detected. On one system, 74 user accounts had privileges enabling them to change program code without supervisory review and approval. This number had increased from the 37 users that we had documented in our earlier review. According to management, only four people should have this authority. On another system, nearly 300 programmers could alter production programs and data.

Segregation of duties refers to the policies, procedures, and organizational structure that help to ensure that one individual cannot independently control all key aspects of a process or computer-related operation and thereby conduct unauthorized actions without detection. As an example, a computer programmer should not be allowed to independently write, test, and approve program changes. In the information processing environment, the duties and access capabilities of systems programmers, application programmers, security administrators, and end-users, for example, should generally be segregated from one another.

Duties in the DoD computing environment were not adequately segregated. We found that personnel were still assigned both systems programming and security administration duties. These individuals could make unauthorized changes to programs and data while using their security privileges to disable the system's capability to create an audit trail of those changes. Thus they could, for example, modify payroll records or shipping records to generate unauthorized payments or to misdirect inventory shipments and suppress the related system audit data to avoid detection.

System software controls limit and monitor access to the powerful programs and sensitive files associated with the computer systems operation. System software helps control and coordinate the input, processing, output, and data storage associated with all of the applications that run on the system. Some system software can change data and program code without creating an audit trail or can be used to modify or delete audit trails.

Improperly configured or poorly maintained system software can be exploited to circumvent security controls to read, modify, or delete critical or sensitive data or programs. It can also be used to gain privileges to conduct unauthorized transactions or to circumvent edits or other controls built into application programs. For these reasons, system software vulnerabilities are a common target of hackers, both internal and external to the entity. As a result, most entities have a separate set of procedures for controlling system software.

We found end-users had been given unnecessary (and in some cases unauthorized) access to system functions, tools, and data. For example, users could read system data files containing information useful to hackers. On four systems, users could view other users' output, which could include sensitive or confidential information. On one system, end-users had the capability to issue commands that would allow them to disrupt all processing on that system. As with other groups of users, the activities and access privileges of users with sensitive system privileges were not adequately monitored.

We also found system software maintenance issues that create security exposures. For example, we found system libraries for privileged programs (i.e., programs that are allowed to perform powerful system functions) that contained the names of nonexistent programs. By creating a new program with the same name as one of these nonexistent members, a user could install malicious code with the authority to make changes to the operating system, the security software, and user programs or data and to delete audit logs. We found that one site was running a proprietary mainframe operating system and other system software products that were no longer supported by the vendor. Management informed us that such software was needed to support application programs that had not yet been upgraded to run on a current version of the operating system. This site was also running programs that were undocumented. These practices increase the risk that security vulnerabilities or other problems will not be detected or corrected.

Service continuity controls ensure that when unexpected events occur, critical operations continue without undue interruption and critical and sensitive data are protected. A well-documented plan for disaster recovery and continuity of operations, based upon an up-to-date risk analysis and periodic testing, is critical to ensure that an organization can continue to fulfill its mission while responding to natural disasters, accidents, or other major and minor interruptions in data processing.

We found mission-related applications and the activities they support that are at risk because of inadequate planning for service continuity. Although DISA recommends nightly back-up of high-activity application data files, some information processing customers did not require that their application data be backed up frequently enough to ensure effective mission support after a service disruption. This increases the risk that some data cannot be restored, particularly as temporary data files may not exist at the time the full system back-up is done, which is typically once a week. Also, although DISA requires that back-up tapes be stored at least 25 miles, and preferably 100 miles, from the processing site, we noted that one DMC was storing back-up tapes only 14 miles from the data center without having obtained a waiver from DISA. This increases the risk that both the back-up tapes and the data center could be affected by the same emergency.

We found that disaster recovery plans were incomplete and did not specify the order in which the customer's applications (or the programs within a particular application) should be restored. This increases the risk that relatively trivial functions may be restored before those that are most critical to the user's mission. One plan assumed the availability of hardware that was not on-site and was still in the procurement process.

Many DISA customers had not tested their recovery procedures or had not tested them under the conditions likely to prevail in the event of a disaster. These weaknesses increase the risk that the organization may fail in its mission or incur unnecessary expense as the result of a prolonged service interruption.

DoD Progress in Addressing Security Weaknesses

GAO has cited DISA's progress in identifying thousands of specific control weaknesses as a major source of progress in DoD organizations. Since DISA created a task force to assess security Defense Megacenters (DMCs) in 1994 it has completed 542 Security Readiness Reviews (SRR), generated a total of 14,860 findings and reported that 11,418 of these findings had been corrected.[103] DISA also began drafting detailed technical guidance for individual systems called Security Technical Implementation Guides (STIG), which give minimum security standards for managing system software security. More specifically, STIGs[104]

cover topics such as organizational relationships and responsibilities and the management processes and technical requirements needed to ensure hardware integrity, system software integrity, and data-level integrity. They define the requirements for interfacing the various components of system software and include such details as specific configuration options to be used, password management, testing requirements, and permissible levels of access to system resources. Most importantly, all DMC systems are subject to SRRs and DMC management is accountable for the findings generated. DISA officials and staff report that correcting SRR deficiencies is given a high priority because the status of SRR findings is a part of each DMC director's or commander readiness report.

At the same time, GAO noted that DISA's publishing of STIGs, while a good first step, is still deficient. Lag time in verification of when corrective actions are reported as completed and actually are completed is a serious oversight problem. Corrective actions are reported as being completed in the SRR database when in fact they may not be verified for several months.[105]

DISA has published STIG's for most of its systems and expects to have performed SRRs of all its systems before the end of 1999. Additional action, however, is needed to improve DISA's oversight of information security. For example, while the DISA's inspector will generally verify any corrective actions taken while he or she is still on site, subsequent corrective actions are reported in the SRR database as having adequately addressed deficiencies even though the actions may not be verified until the next regularly scheduled inspection, which may be 15 to 36 months later. We found this practice has resulted in some inaccuracies. We tested 55 deficiencies that were "accepted-as-fixed" in the SRR database and determined that about one-fourth had not been corrected. For example, several DMCs had reported that their system software configuration options had been changed to conform to DISA requirements, and the SRR database had been updated accordingly. However, our testing showed that the options in question were not in compliance with DISA standards. We did not attempt to determine whether these inconsistencies were the result of oversights, misrepresentations, or other factors. DISA officials agreed more timely, independent verification of corrective actions is desirable and reported that they were exploring ways to address the issue.

Other DoD components had not made similar progress in instituting an effective oversight process. The modest improvements that these components had made were a result of individual and isolated command or unit actions rather than comprehensive service, agency, or department actions.

GAO reported that overall the DoD has developed but not yet implemented a department-wide information security program. In 1996, GAO made several recommendations to DoD after it found that the department "lacked a department-wide security program to comprehensively address the general control weaknesses we had identified." DoD concurred with these recommendations and issued plans for a Defense-wide Information Assurance Program (DIAP) which would "provide the framework for a comprehensive information security program. As of the 1999 report GAO found that it was too early to assess how effective DIAP management and implementation plans have been implemented and whether or not DIAP's efforts would ensure adequate information security.[106]

Cyber and Information Warfare and the Role of the Intelligence Community

Most intelligence community offensive cyber-activity is highly classified, and should be. There are no public breakdowns of federal spending on intelligence activity related to the defense of critical infrastructure, no unclassified assessments, and few useful leaks. At the same time, there are enough anecdotal reports to raise important questions.

- *Who is in charge of intelligence collection on foreign threats to the nation's critical infrastructure and information systems?* The issue here is not the designation of responsibility per se, but function capability. It simply is not clear that there is functional capability to carry out the necessary tasks, suitable coordination and information flow, and close communication with users. Recent reorganization efforts within the community attempt to address this problem, but the verdict is still not in on whether they are successful.

- *Is there sufficient coordination within the intelligence community and flow to users?* Virtually all intelligence agency personnel privately complain about a lack of adequate coordination within the intelligence community, particularly about the flow of information from NSA, or leaks and misuse of information shared with federal law enforcement by the community. Many such complaints, however, seem to be parochial, and many user complaints seem to stem from poor user tasking and prioritization. The Gulf War, Kosovo, and areas like missile threat analysis have revealed serious problems in these areas, but it is not clear what problems specifically affect the problem of critical infrastructure protection.

- *Does the community have the necessary resources?* The numbers and quality of technical personnel seem to be inadequate, primarily because adequate funding often does not go to technical expertise and capability. There is heavy dependence on contractors under conditions where contract awards and management often seem to be poorly handled and involve long delays and misuse of the resulting work effort. Additionally, the bureaucracy of the community is prone to running IO/IW related projects for internal political reasons rather than to acquire specific useable intelligence or develop capability. Anecdotally, the community seemingly suffers from poor morale in its IO/IW analytic community because of poor training and career opportunities, and a lack of understanding of the work by the recipients of the analysis.

- *What is the responsibility of the intelligence community to wage offensive warfare?* The war in Kosovo showed that the intelligence community still had many of the coordination problems exposed during the Cold War. More than that, it indicated that the natural collection and analysis bias of the intelligence community meant that it was not ready to wage offensive information warfare even against a local and relatively weak opponent. The intelligence community often proposes the use of aggressive information warfare at games and exercises, but many proposals reveal a theoretical or conceptual understanding of the role such warfare might play that is not supported by technical expertise. There are indications that the community is better prepared to "talk the talk" than "digitize the digits." It is also often far from clear that the community and U.S. military are effectively organized to coordinate in such actions.

- *What are the special responsibilities of the CIA and NSA?* It is unclear from the open literature that the federal government has yet conducted a zero-based review of the role the nation's key intelligence agencies must play in dealing with cyber-threats, although there are indications that such a review may be underway at NSA. Once again, the issue is not assigning responsibility or creating organizational structures, but one of determining exactly what capabilities are needed and ensuring that they are properly staffed and funded.

- *The risk of deep management and conceptual failures within the intelligence community.* It is dangerous to try to assess the adequacy of the efforts of agencies like NSA, and the many other intelligence efforts dealing with information warfare, from the outside and without full access to classified information. At the same time, it is far from clear that NSA and other members of the intelligence community have the personnel, technology, and resources to carry out their information warfare and cyber-attack/ defense missions. It is also far from clear that there has been sufficient net assessment of the trends in technology, the growth of private sector use of advanced information systems, and intelligence collection and analysis resources to determine how NSA and other relevant intelligence agency efforts will cope in the future. It is at least possible that the capability of national technical means will slowly erode over time or require major unprogrammed investment.

- *Has a proper net technology assessment been conducted to support intelligence planning and programming?* Much of the community activity seems to be centered around concepts that are not supported by a coherent view of the present and probable technical capabilities of our allies and opponents, and the balance of offensive and defensive technology. It is unclear that programs and activities must be evaluated in these terms, or that program goals and milestones are based on such an evaluation.

- *Do adequate laws and regulations exist to allow the proper coordination between intelligence and law enforcement?* There seem to be serious problems in ensuring the kind of near real-time exchange of data needed between the intelligence community, law enforcement, and those under attack. Legal problems exist at one level because of the risk of spying on U.S. citizens, and at another level because law enforcement agencies often cannot or will not report on ongoing investigations or cases before a grand jury or trial. Failings in this area seem to have impeded progress on high profile cases such as Solar Sunrise and Moonlight Maze by increasing response time and creating inadvertent counter-intelligence problems. Other problems, such as information sharing within the intelligence community, are exacerbated by a lack of standard interpretations of the law. Some agencies use more flexible interpretations than others—causing some agencies to reject information from others, and worse—causes analysts and other operatives to be increasingly cautious about their activity to the detriment of operational effectiveness.

- *Does the community effectively coordinate technical and operational development with relevant private sector entities?* The intelligence community, like all government organizations, is hard pressed to keep pace with rapidly developing information technology. Many private enterprises in the U.S. and abroad are the manufacturers of the hardware and software that makes networked information systems function, and they have a vested interest in ensuring the robust security and reliability of their products, just as the intelligence community does. To maintain necessary capabilities, the intelligence community should be working with private enterprise to help maintain its edge and improve capabilities in critical areas such as attribution of attackers and analysis of new attacks and vulnerabilities. So far, little evidence can be found to indicate that the intelligence community is building these kinds of relationships.

Total Spending on National Security Activity

The OMB estimate of total national security agency spending on critical infrastructure protection is also shown in Table 4.5. There is no indication of the extent to which this activity relates to offensive and retaliatory capabilities in cyber-warfare, and the level of preparation for asymmetric attacks by states, their proxies, and major terrorist groups versus lower levels of attack. Similarly, no data are available on NSA plans to maintain and improve national collection capabilities in this area, and whether or not technical assessments have been performed to estimate future NSA capability (or that of any other element of the national security community).

Department of State

The OMB reporting on the State Department's role in critical infrastructure protection does not provide a detailed description. The GAO reported in May 1998, however, that its tests on State computer systems were "very susceptible to hackers, terrorists, or other unauthorized individuals seeking to damage State operations or reap financial gain by exploiting the department's information security weaknesses."[107]

An independent accounting firm reported in August 1999 that the Department of State's mainframe computers for domestic operations were vulnerable to unauthorized access. "Consequently, other systems, which process data using these computers, could also be vulnerable."

Department of Transportation

The DOT is lead federal agency for protecting the transportation sector from both physical and cyber-threats and has had significant funding, especially in FY2001 where $99.34 million has been requested for

CIP protection. A total of $97 million of the requested FY2001 budget is slated for public CIP assistance. Another $60.45 million is allocated in the budget for threat, vulnerability and assessments, an increase from the $29.33 enacted in FY2000.

Department of Treasury

The Treasury is the lead federal agency in banking and finance. Treasury is scheduled to receive $87.03 million for CIP efforts in the FY2001 budget. Of this money, $4 million is to go to research and development into "authentication technologies; physical and electronic protection technologies; test facilities; simulation model development information security analysis; intrusion indications and warning tools system reliability enhancement; information system standardization; electronic commerce security enhancement."[108] Another $7 million is to go to protecting Public Key Infrastructures (PKI).

Department of Veterans Affairs

The Department of Veterans spends the majority of the $17.33 million in FY2000 and $17.39 million requested in FY2001 on systems protection. ($15.6 in FY2000 and $15.65 in FY2001).[109] The rest is spent on education and training and threat assessments.

According to an October 1999 GAO report, "serious weaknesses placed sensitive information belonging to the Department of Veterans Affairs at risk of inadvertent or deliberate misuse, fraudulent use, improper disclosure, or destruction, possible occurring without detection." GAO writes that such findings were disturbing because "VA collects and maintains sensitive medical record and benefit payment information for veterans and family members and is responsible for tens of billions of dollars of benefit payments annually."[110]

Chapter 5

Assessments of Effectiveness

There are only a relatively limited number of detailed assessments of the current federal effort. There are, however, a number of reports that provide considerable insight into its problems and success, and there are a number of issues that clearly need to be addressed.

INDEPENDENT U.S. GOVERNMENT EFFORTS TO ASSESS RISK, COST, AND BENEFITS: GAO TESTIMONY OF OCTOBER 6, 1999

In a testimony before the Senate Subcommittee on Technology, Terrorism, and Government Information, Committee on the Judiciary in October 6, 1999, Jack L. Brock, Director of the Government-wide and Defense Information Systems Accounting and Information Management Division discussed the fundamental improvements needed to assure the security of federal information systems. According to Brock, the GAO audits had found that 22 of the largest federal agencies have "significant security weaknesses." These audits show that the government "is not adequately protecting critical federal operations and assets from computer-based attacks." From this determination, the GAO found that "addressing this widespread and persistent problem requires significant management attention and action within individual agencies as well as increased coordination and oversight at the government-wide level."

Brock goes on to relate details of the weaknesses found by the GAO audits which highlighted government-wide security weaknesses in controls over access to systems, software development and changes and continuity of service plans.

> GAO and IG reports issued over the last 5 years describe persistent computer security weaknesses that place federal operations such as national defense, law enforcement, air traffic control, and benefit payments at risk of disruption as well as fraud and inappropriate disclosures. Our most recent analysis, of reports issued during fiscal year 1999, identified significant computer security weaknesses in (1) controls over access to sensitive systems and data, (2) controls over software development and changes, and (3) continuity of service plans. These types of weaknesses increase the risk that intruders or authorized users with malicious intentions could read, modify, delete, or otherwise damage information or disrupt operations for purposes, such as fraud, sabotage, or espionage. This body of audit evidence led us, in February 1997 and again in January 1999, to designate information security as a government-wide high risk area in reports to Congress.

Brock then offered the following examples in NASA, DoD, DOA, and Veterans Affairs:

> In May 1999, we reported that, as part of our test of the National Aeronautics and Space Administration's (NASA) computer-based controls, we successfully penetrated several mission-critical systems. Having obtained access, we could have disrupted NASA's ongoing command and control operations and stolen, modified, or destroyed system software and data.
>
> In August 1999, we reported that serious weaknesses in the Department of Defense (DoD) information security continue to provide both hackers and hundreds of thousands of authorized users the opportunity to modify, steal, inappropriately disclose, and destroy sensitive DoD data. These weaknesses impair DoD's ability to (1) control physical and electronic access to its systems and data, (2) ensure that software running on its systems is properly authorized, tested, and functioning as intended. (3) limit employees' ability to perform incompatible functions, and (4) resume operations in the event of a disaster. As a result, numerous Defense functions, including weapons and supercomputer research, logistics, finance, procurement, personnel management, military health, and payroll, have already been adversely affected by system attacks or fraud.
>
> In July 1999, we reported that the Department of Agriculture's (USDA) National Finance Center (NFC) had serious access control weaknesses that affected its ability to prevent and/or detect unauthorized changes to payroll and other payment data or computer software. NFC develops and

operates administrative and financial systems, including payroll/personnel, property management, and accounting systems for both the USDA and more than 60 other federal organizations. During fiscal year 1998, NFC processed more than $19 billion in payroll payments for more than 450,000 federal employees. NFC is also responsible for maintaining records for the world's largest 401(k)-type program, the federal Thrift Savings Program. This program, which is growing at about $1 billion per month, covers about 2.3 million employees and totaled more than $60 billion as of September 30, 1998. The weaknesses we identified increased the risk that users could cause improper payments and that sensitive information could be misused, improperly disclosed, or destroyed.

In October 1999, we reported that Department of Veterans Affairs (VA) systems continued to be vulnerable to unauthorized access. VA operates the largest healthcare delivery system in the United States and reported spending more than $17 billion on medical care in fiscal year 1998. The department also processed more than 42 million benefits payments totaling about $22 billion in fiscal year 1998 and provided life insurance protection through more than 2.4 million policies that represented about $23 billion in coverage. In providing these benefits and services, VA collects and maintains sensitive medical record and benefit payment information for veterans and their family members. GAO, as well as the VA IG, continued to find serious problems that placed sensitive information at increased risk of inadvertent or deliberate misuse, fraudulent use, improper disclosure, or destruction, possibly occurring without detection. For example, at one VA insurance center, 265 users who had not been authorized access had the ability to read, write, and delete information related to insurance awards. Such unauthorized access could lead to improper insurance payments.

In addition to control problems Brock cited poor security management as the fundamental cause of poor computer security. Caused partly by a lack of understanding of risks, staff shortages, lack of security architectures, and poor security management, Brock also highlights the lack of awareness on the part of high-level agency officials who have traditionally left information security to lower-level technical specialists. Brock says that:

> While a number of factors have contributed to weak federal information security, such as insufficient understanding of risks, technical staff shortages, and a lack of system and security architectures, the fundamental underlying problem is poor security program management. We reported this problem in 1996, and, again, in 1998, noting that agency managers are not ensuring, on an ongoing basis, that risks are identified and addressed and that controls are operating as intended. In many cases, senior agency officials have not recognized that computer-supported operations

are integral to carrying out their missions and that they can no longer relegate the security of these operations solely to lower-level technical specialists. For these reasons, it is essential that this fundamental problem be addressed as part of an effective information technology management strategy, which will also serve to strengthen critical infrastructure protection.

Brock's testimony goes on to relate that even when agencies have responded to recommendations from either the GAO or agency inspector generals, the weaknesses continue to resurface as a result of the lack of a management framework for "overseeing information security on an agency-wide and ongoing basis." Basically, the GAO's main criticism of agencies in this case is their inability to see the big picture security-wise. So even though they may respond to individual audits, another problem resurfaces that may have been seen if the system was looked at holistically.

Management Recommendations Within Brock's Testimony

Brock mentions another GAO report in which eight nonfederal organizations, which were known for having superior security programs, were studied to obtain trends in the way they managed their information security. According to Brock the report found that these companies manage their systems "through a cycle of risk management activities." Built on 16 specific practices, the basic framework "allows risk management through an ongoing cycle of activities coordinated by a central focal point. The management process involves assessing risk to determine information security needs, developing and implementing policies and controls that meet these needs, promoting awareness to ensure that risks, roles, and responsibilities are understood, and instituting an ongoing program of test and evaluations to ensure that policies and controls are appropriate and effective."

The GAO indicated seven key areas that could help the government provide better assurance for critical infrastructure objectives.

Clearly Defined Roles and Responsibilities

First, it is important that the federal strategy delineate the roles and responsibilities of the numerous entities involved in federal information security and related aspects of critical infrastructure protection. Under current law, OMB is responsible for overseeing and coordinating federal agency security; and the National Institute of Standards and Technology (NIST), with assistance from the National Security Agency (NSA), is responsible for establishing related standards. In addition, interagency bodies, such as the CIO Council and the entities created under PDD-63 are attempting to coordinate agency initiatives.

While these organizations have developed fundamentally sound policies and guidance and have undertaken potentially useful initiatives, effective improvements are not taking place. This is due, in part, to the relative immaturity of the recently established processes. It is also unclear how the activities of these many organizations interrelate, who should be held accountable for their success or failure, and whether they will effectively and efficiently support national goals.

Constraints on resources and the urgency of the problem require that government activities are designed and coordinated to achieve clearly understood goals. There must also be clear linkage between policy guidance, technical standards, and agency practices to ensure responsibility/accountability for actual improvements.

With regards to NIST efforts with NSA, these efforts are virtually unknown within U.S. Government circles. In fact, these efforts are almost unknown even within the parts of the NIST organization which are responsible for NIST computer and network security. NIST itself has made, or has come close to making, poor decisions about their own network security. For example, it came close to choosing a firewall product produced in a foreign country that is known within the community to have been compromised by that source country's government. Given that NSA performed the assurance testing on this product and detected its flaws, it seems that either the security apparatus at NIST was never made aware of information available to the internal effort referenced here, or that effort was never provided sufficient information by NSA. The latter isn't at all out of the question, as NSA puts excessive controls on information in order to maintain its importance within the Intelligence Community at the expense of the rest of the community, as well as the government as a whole. In summation, NIST's efforts are nearly anonymous, whatever reporting and recommendations they have made are very poorly disseminated. Furthermore, they have extremely limited access to classified materials on the subject matter, have personnel without sufficient awareness of the threat, and/or some combination thereof.

Specific Risk-based Standards

Second, agencies need more specific guidance on the controls that they need to implement. Currently agencies have wide discretion in deciding (1) what computer security controls to implement and (2) the level of rigor with which they enforce these controls. In theory, this is appropriate since, as OMB and NIST guidance states, the level of protection that agencies provide should be commensurate with the risk to agency operations and assets. In essence, one set of specific controls will not be appropriate for all types of systems and data.

However, our studies of best practices at leading organizations have shown that more specific guidance is important. In particular, specific mandatory standards for varying risk levels can clarify expectations for information protection, including audit criteria; provide a standard framework for assessing information security risk; and help ensure that shared data are appropriately protected. Implementing such standards for federal agencies would require developing (1) a single set of information classification categories for use by all agencies to define the criticality and sensitivity of the various types of information they maintain and (2) minimum mandatory requirements for protecting information in each classification category.

More specific guidance is absolutely critical for several reasons not listed here.

First, one of the major problems with government networks is that poor security at seemingly non-critical agencies creates access paths by which anyone can attack another agency's systems while seemingly coming from a fellow agency. Since current law seemingly handicaps Intelligence Community and Law Enforcement efforts when they cross national borders into the United States, this makes it difficult to pursue attackers by making attribution extremely difficult. The first hurdle it creates is that it requires inter-agency cooperation for information to be shared effectively about the intrusion. And second, it raises the possibility that the attack comes from a U.S. citizen, immediately removing the IC from the equation until such time as LE discovers that this was merely a stopping point for a foreign attack.

Additionally, sensitive infrastructure information is not closely held at agencies that do not have a history of protecting and compartmentalizing information. Agencies that handle things like civilian mapping of coastal waters and whatnot may not see that information as sensitive, but a foreign adversary would certainly find it useful.

Finally, to preempt a counter argument from the places that tend to have lax security, it is perfectly possible to create (and require) secure access pathways which simultaneously protect the freedom of action which most senior staff and research types prefer while also securing systems from outside intrusion. And this can be done nearly seamlessly with COTS products—products that would be better and easier to use if an organization as large as the USG were added to the demand-pull.

Network security is critical at every agency.

Routine Evaluations of Agency Performance

Third, routine periodic audits must be implemented to allow for meaningful performance measurement. A requirement for periodic examinations of controls in operation would significantly strengthen oversight requirements in the Computer Security Act, which focus on evaluating agency security plans, rather than practices. Under this proposed recommendation audits would be used to determine if security goals are met and if policies and controls put in place are operating as intended. At the time of the testimony, there is no requirement for periodic independently initiated evaluations and to complete such a change legislation would be needed.

Ensuring effective implementation of agency information security and critical infrastructure protection plans will require monitoring to determine if milestones are being met and testing to determine if policies and controls are operating as intended. Evaluations at several levels can be beneficial. Tests initiated by agency officials are essential because they provide information needed to fulfill their ongoing responsibility for managing security programs. Evaluations initiated by independent auditors, such as agency inspectors general, can serve as an independent check on management evaluations and provide useful information for congressional and executive branch oversight. Summary evaluations performed by entities such as OMB, GAO, or the CIO Council can provide a government-wide view of progress and help identify crosscutting problems.

At present, there is no requirement for periodic independently initiated tests and evaluations of agency computer security programs. As a result, information for measuring the effectiveness of agency security programs, and thus, holding agency managers accountable is limited. While some control testing is done in support of annual independent financial statement audits, ensuring routine periodic testing of all critical agency systems—both financial and nonfinancial—may require new legislation.

Executive Branch and Congressional Oversight

Fourth, the executive branch and the Congress must effectively use audit results and performance measures to monitor agency performance and take whatever action is deemed advisable to remedy identified problems. Such oversight is essential to hold agencies accountable for their performance and was demonstrated by the recent OMB and congressional efforts to oversee the Year 2000 challenge.

Adequate Technical Expertise

Fifth, it is important for agencies to have the technical expertise they need to select, implement, and maintain controls that protect their computer systems. Similarly, the federal government must maximize the value of its technical staff by sharing expertise and information. The Computer Security Act authorized NIST to provide assistance to agencies and included provisions for periodic training in computer security awareness and practice. However, as the Year 2000 challenge showed, the availability of adequate technical expertise has been a continuing concern to agencies.

A number of programs and recommendations have been proposed that merit congressional study. For example, prompted in part by concerns over technical staff shortages affecting Year 2000 efforts, the CIO Council's Education and Training committee studied ways to help agencies recruit and retain information technology personnel. The resulting report provides an extensive description of the current status of federal information technology employment, improvement efforts currently underway, and detailed proposals for action.

Adequate Funding

Sixth, agencies must have resources sufficient to support their computer security and infrastructure protection activities. Funding for security is already embedded to some extent in agency budgets for computer system development efforts and routine network and system management and maintenance. However, some additional amounts are likely to be needed to address specific weaknesses and new tasks. Also, addressing the Year 2000 challenge has resulted in postponement of many program and information technology initiatives—including system enhancements and computer security. OMB and congressional oversight of future spending on computer security will be important to ensure that agencies are not using the funds they receive to continue ad hoc, piece-meal security fixes not supported by a strong agency risk management framework.

It should be noted that funding within the Intelligence Community for the outside help that it desperately needs seems increasingly tight at every agency, raising the question of where supposed increases in funding are going.

Incident Response and Coordination

Seventh, there is a need to more comprehensively monitor and develop responses to intrusions, viruses, and other incidents that threaten federal systems. Several entities are already providing some central coordination in this area—including the FBI, NIST, and the FedCIRC. However, the specific roles and responsibilities of these organizations, as well as the balance between government-wide and individual agency responsibilities, should be clarified and expanded to provide a more comprehensive picture of the security events that are occurring and assistance in dealing with them.

Such efforts can take several forms that provide differing benefits. For example, a government-wide response center could provide immediate emergency assistance to agencies experiencing intrusions or other potential problems. It could also provide assistance on a non-emergency basis, especially by alerting agencies to new threats and vulnerabilities and helping them identify actions to prevent or mitigate incidents. By calling on a center for such assistance, agencies could tap into a source of specialized expertise that may be difficult and expensive to maintain at the individual agency level. A government-wide center could also serve as clearinghouse of information on incidents that would be available to federal agencies and the public. Such information can be valuable in estimating the significance of different types of information security risks. For example, when the Melissa virus surfaced earlier this year, we found that there was no single place to obtain complete data on what agencies were hit and how they were affected. Moreover, there were no data available that quantified the impact of the virus in terms of productivity lost or the value of data lost.

Finally, it is important to recognize that, by itself, a central clearinghouse is not complete solution for the information security problems across the federal government. Agencies themselves must still use this information effectively to assess risks to their own computer-supported operations and to develop and implement sound management controls.

INDEPENDENT U.S. GOVERNMENT EFFORTS TO ASSESS RISK, COST, AND BENEFITS: GAO TESTIMONY OF MARCH 29, 2000

On March 29, 2000, in a testimony before the House Subcommittee on Government Management, Information and Technology, Brock made remarks similar to his testimony made in 1999. In addition to the weaknesses he mentioned about DoD, NASA, and Veteran's Affairs he added State Department vulnerabilities.

Weaknesses in Controls

Brock listed control weaknesses as being at the center of federal computer system vulnerabilities. These control weaknesses included entity-wide security program planning and management, access controls, application software development and change controls, and segregation of duties, system software controls, and service continuity controls.[111]

Entity-wide Security Program Planning and Management: Each organization needs a set of management procedures and an organizational framework for identifying and assessing risks, deciding what policies and controls are needed, periodically evaluating the effectiveness of these policies and controls, and acting to address any identified weaknesses. These are the fundamental activities that allow an organization to manage its information security risks cost effectively, rather than reacting to individual problems ad hoc only after a violation has been detected or an audit finding has been reported. Despite the importance of this aspect of an information security program, we continue to find that poor security planning and management is the rule rather than the exception. Most agencies do not develop security plans for major systems based on risk, have not formally documented security policies and have not implemented programs for testing and evaluating the effectiveness of the controls they rely on.

Access Controls: Access controls limit or detect inappropriate access to computer resources (data, equipment, and facilities) thereby protecting these resources against unauthorized modification, loss, and disclosure. They include physical protections such as gates and guards. They also include logical controls, which are controls built into software that (1) require users to authenticate themselves through passwords or other identifiers and (2) limit the files and other resources that an authenticated user can access and the actions that he or she can execute. In many of our reviews we have found that managers do not identify or document access needs for individual users or groups, and, as a result, they provide overly broad access privileges to very large groups of users. Additionally, we often find that users share accounts and passwords or post passwords in plain view, making it impossible to trace specific transactions or modifications to an individual. Unfortunately, as a result of these and other access control weaknesses, auditors conducting penetration tests of agency systems are almost always successful in gaining unauthorized access that would allow intruders to read, modify, or delete data for whatever purposes they had in mind.

Application Software Development and Change Controls: Application software development and change controls prevent unauthorized software programs or modifications to programs from being implemented. Without them, individuals can surreptitiously modify software programs to include processing steps or features that could later be exploited for personal gain or sabotage. In many of our audits, we find that (1) testing procedures are undisciplined and do not ensure that implemented software operates as intended, (2) implementation procedures do not ensure that only authorized software is used, and (3) access to software program libraries is inadequately controlled.

Segregation of Duties: Segregation of duties refers to the policies, procedures, and organizational structure that help ensure that one individual cannot independently control all key aspects of a process computer-related operation and thereby conduct unauthorized actions or gain unauthorized access to assets or records without detection. For example, one computer programmer should not be allowed to independently write, test, and approve program changes. We commonly find that computer programmers and operators are authorized to perform a wide variety of duties, thus providing them the ability to independently modify, circumvent, and disable system security features. Similarly, we have also identified problems related to transaction processing, where all users of a financial management system can independently perform all of the steps needed to initiate and complete a payment.

System Software Controls: System software controls limit and monitor access to the powerful programs and sensitive files associated with the computer systems operation, e.g., operating systems, system utilities, security software, and database management systems. If controls in this area are inadequate, unauthorized individuals might use system software to circumvent security controls to read, modify, or delete critical or sensitive information and programs. Such weaknesses seriously diminish the reliability of information produced by all of the applications supported by the computer system and increase the risk of fraud, sabotage, and inappropriate disclosures. Our reviews frequently identify systems with insufficiently restricted access that in turn makes it possible for knowledgeable individuals to disable or circumvent controls.

Service Continuity Controls: Service continuity controls ensure that critical operations can continue when unexpected events occur, such as a temporary power failure, accidental loss of files, or even a major disaster such as a fire. For this reason, an agency should have (1) procedures in place to protect information resources and minimize the risk of unplanned interruptions and (2) a plan to recover critical operations should interruptions occur. At many of the agencies we have reviewed, we have found that plans and procedures are incomplete because operations and supporting resources had not been fully analyzed to determine which were most critical and would need to be restored first. In addition, disaster recovery plans are often not fully tested to identify their weaknesses. As a result, many agencies have inadequate assurance that they can recover operational capability in a timely, orderly manner after a disruptive attack.

As the suggestions made in earlier testimony, the GAO recommendations to deal with this lack of controls centered on a similar track. According to Brock, the GAO listed six actions agencies can take to address weaknesses in controls. The actions listed were increase awareness, ensure that existing controls are operating effectively, ensure that software patches are up to date, use automated scanning and testing tools to quickly identify problems, propagate their best practices, and ensure that their most common vulnerabilities are addressed. Brock stated that while these actions alone would not ensure good security, "they take advantage of readily available information tools and, thus, do not involve significant new resources. As a result, they are steps that can be made without delay."[112]

Raise Awareness

Brock called for the raised awareness on the part of senior government executives. Brock stated that the GAO found that when high-level individuals do not understand the importance of information security risk "they may not devote adequate resources to security or be willing to tolerate the inconvenience that may be associated with maintaining adequate controls."[113] In these statements and the statements made earlier, the GAO emphasized the importance of agency information security from the top all the way down the chain of command. For this to happen, the GAO felt that top agency executives must be well informed of risks and vulnerabilities.

The GAO's recommendations also stressed the importance of implementing policy controls effectively. "Policies and controls are no good if they are not maintained properly." The GAO suggested that "agencies must take steps to examine or test key controls routinely and enforce compliance with policies."[114]

Implement Software Patches

The GAO asserted the importance of updating the latest software patches to decrease vulnerabilities. According to GAO audits, it found that patches were not installed promptly or at all leaving vulnerabilities in agency systems. To avoid this the GAO suggested "(1) keeping system administrators aware of the latest software vulnerability alerts and the related remedial actions that need to be taken and (2) ensuring that needed patches are implemented promptly."[115]

This recommendation presents problems of its own. The key problem in many organizations is not a lack of awareness of patches but rather the fact that they cannot implement patches until they are given express permission to do so. Many system administrators also look at the unknown bugs that will come with a new patch and ask whether it is not better to stick with known ones and wait. Problems can also occur because on occasion patch releases are so bad that they are rejected wholesale by these same system administrators, but are forcibly implemented by regulations requiring that patches be kept up to date. For example, Windows NT Service pack 6 caused numerous stability problems and many refused to update to it until the patch itself was patched to version 6A.

Routinely Use Automated Tools to Monitor Security

The fourth recommendation was that agencies use readily available software tools such as scanners, which search for system vulnerabilities; password cracking tools, which test password strength; network monitoring tools used to monitor system configurations and network traffic, which can identify unusual or suspicious network activity. Brock warned that the use of these tools must be carefully managed to make sure they are not misused or improperly managed.[116]

While automated intrusion detection and network auditing tools are helpful, they can contribute to the passive posture that keeps the government perpetually on the defensive and cannot be relied upon by themselves to ensure the security of mission-critical systems. Nevertheless, extremely effective tools are in the public domain, such as USNSWC-Dahlgren's "SHADOW" (Secondary Heuristic Analysis and Detection for Online Warfare), and other excellent free network auditing tools such as SAINT and NESSUS are not used extensively. This occurs in spite of the fact that these are the same tools used by many low-grade attackers to profile targets.

Identify and Propagate Pockets of Excellence

This recommendation called for agencies to expand upon good practices that are already in place. GAO audit reports have shown that "even agencies with poor security programs often have good practices in certain areas of their security programs or certain organizational units." The GAO points to central coordination as a way to identify pockets of excellence and propagate them to an agency or agencies.[117] Implementation is much harder work than writing a mandate. These kinds of problems sometimes remain unsolved because of systemic fear of taking unilateral action within the government. Without clear mandates of authority within an organization, no center of excellence can propagate its skills. Management, ever fearful of a mistake when faced with technical issues beyond their scope, is extremely risk averse about trying to share and accept expertise from other agencies.

Focus on the Most Common Vulnerabilities First

Recognizing commonly found vulnerabilities and distributing them on lists followed by suggested corrective actions is suggested by the GAO as a way for agencies to share information in an in-house or across-agency manner. This could in turn allow technical experts to work on more difficult problems while reducing agency risks.[118]

Enforce a Strong Management Approach

To make for lasting improvement efforts the GAO advocates the creation of strong management frameworks to ensure that agency actions are appropriately controlled and coordinated testing tools are appropriately selected and tested prior to their use, and personnel involved in using tools and in implementing software patches are properly trained. Good practices and lessons are shared on an agency-wide basis, controls are systematically tested to ensure that they are effective, and appropriate risk management decisions are made regarding the best way to address identified problems.[119]

The GAO states that this required that agencies take a comprehensive approach involving senior agency program managers who understand which aspects of their missions are the most critical and sensitive and technical experts who know the agencies systems and can suggest appropriate technical security control techniques. Again Brock mentioned the "Learning From Leading Organizations" report and recounted the findings mentioned earlier in this report.

PRELIMINARY ANALYSIS OF GAO FINDINGS

The GAO findings indicate that the U.S. government lags behind both administration goals and information security expectations. If the GAO audits are correct federal agencies continue to fail at even the most basic levels of computer security, whether it be people sharing or openly posting passwords or too many people having too much access. At this rate, any idea of the federal government being a model of "best practices" seems like a pipe dream.

At the same time, many of the GAO's complaints about unauthorized personnel having administrative system privileges are not functional. Even with just one project running on a system, problems can be encountered regularly that cost administrators inordinate amounts of time by forcing them to deal with problems that are best left to users. These problems are prevalent because they are most easily circumvented by giving people higher levels of access than they normally need. The best solution to the problem of inappropriate access levels being granted is to develop better tools and operating environments so that constant little changes that require administrator privileges are no longer required.

Compounding this issue, according to GAO findings, the government is at a significant disadvantage due to the lack of technical manpower in the federal ranks. The administration seems to be recognizing this and the GAO gives them credit for seeking to establish programs to develop highly trained computer science and information security personnel. Still, it remains to be seen if the government can draw the best computer personnel away from extremely lucrative jobs in private industry. Technical manpower within the ranks of many key offices is acutely limited.

NIPC and other key organizations are sometimes highly dependent on outside help, and do not have the funding to secure additional help.

For approaches to providing adequate information security for the federal government, the GAO seems to follow a few themes in their recommendations. On a government-wide level the GAO favors standards and the sharing of information security best practices and the propagation of common approaches across government. Security control standards is another area of GAO recommendation concern. The GAO has found that agencies have not done well at evaluating risk and implementing controls. For this reason the GAO would like to see more guidance in the form of data classifications, which would establish minimum security requirements for each classification of materials.[120]

The GAO places an important part of the success of information security risk management on the shoulders of the agency managers themselves, especially those at the highest level. The GAO seems to be of the opinion that if high-level officials are aware of information security risk and are serious about them, then information security will be taken seriously. This top-down priority approach to agency information security could work to change lax security cultures and habits within agencies. Also on the government-wide level having strong centralized management and the support of officials in government and in Congress could enhance information security. The GAO cites the Y2K preparations as an example of this coalition being formed to address a problem. The GAO advocates the creation of a national chief information officer to "provide higher visibility and more effective central leadership of information security."[121]

Being the auditors that it is, the GAO favors strongly the adoption of rigorous and frequent information security audits of agencies, to monitor how they are doing in relation to meeting their information security goals. More rigorous audits seem like an appropriate and commonsense response to a fast paced and ever changing technology field.

OTHER EFFORTS TO ASSESS RISK, COST, AND BENEFITS

Experts in the executive branch have developed a great deal of insight into the overall quality of the federal effort that has not been provided in detailed reports. They report that audits within the national security agencies are generally adequate, but that most civil agencies fall short of adequate review and performance. These experts cite the following major problems in the federal effort:

- *Secretaries and top officials do not take personal responsibility and are not held accountable.* Responsibility is effectively pushed down upon the Chief Information Officer, who is usually underfunded, understaffed, and over-tasked. The CIO is not given budget review authority or sufficient support to force adequate performance and lacks the resources to conduct adequate review.

- *While responsibility is tasked by OMB, as part of A-130, the practical reality is that Congress refuses to appropriate extra money and the Chief Financial Officer refuses to allocate adequate resources out of the existing budget.* The CIO is given an impossible job, and managers lack resources.

- *Basic technical expertise is lacking.* Training funds are not adequate and even the CIO and the CIO's staff are generally so heavily engaged in day-to-day work that they have no time for training. Managers and technical personnel often lack basic expertise—many CIO's have no specialized background and special competence—and cannot perform the required tasks. Good CIO's have strong incentives to leave and their staffs tend to be in their 40s with far too limited a cadre of younger technical experts.

- *Federal pay is inadequate.* Competent personnel can easily earn 100-150% more outside the government, with more training, authority, and access to cutting edge technology. Agencies have the legal authority to spend more, but CFO's refuse to spend the funds. The end result is a selection out process where the incompetent tend to stay and competent tend to leave.

- *Annual audits are either not carried out or are largely cosmetic.* GAO audits do lead to temporary improvements, but these effects are not sustained because all departments and agencies are not subject to annual audits.

- *Emergency response capabilities often involves voice coordination, rather than automated response.* This seems to be true even at the overall federal level, where emergencies have to be dealt with largely by telephone. The exception is the Department of Defense Joint Task Force which also has an automatic patch and data exchange capability.

- *The failures in prevention are accompanied by far greater failures in re-constitution and mitigation.* The present federal effort funds prevention with little regard to reconstitution and mitigation. The federal plan and federal audits do not properly deal with this issue. FEMA has declared it has no role in reconstitution. Red teams test such capabilities only in part of the national security community.

There is no more reason to assume that federal entities will take proper responsibility for critical infrastructure and cyber-protection than there is to assume they can be trusted to control the efficiency of their accounting and audit procedures. Moreover, the pace of technology change is so rapid that it is not reasonable to assume that most departments and agencies can develop the necessary competence to assess every aspect of their vulnerability. There is a need to either charge the GAO with annual audits of all federal agencies and departments, or to create a federal agency or office charged with the independent auditing of the success of federal efforts to ensure critical infrastructure protection of computer/information systems. It should also be clear that the secretary or head of a department or agency will have personal responsibility for its performance, and that the chief financial officer will have equal responsibility with the chief information officer.

Finally, the federal government must decide how to provide the proper degree of central control for its efforts. There is broad agreement that some central office is needed to coordinate the federal effort, to ensure proper auditing and capability, and to coordinate emergency response capability. There is also broad agreement that such a coordinator needs sufficient rank and authority to speak for the President on these issues, and to ensure that agency budget submissions must include adequate programs and funding. At present, the NSC lacks the staff, funding, and focus to carry out these tasks, and no amount of effort can create a coordinated federal effort without central direction. NIPC, which is charged with central coordination on this issue, is plagued with similar problems, and is additionally handicapped by a contentious relationship between DOJ and other agencies.

TECHNICAL RISKS, TESTS, AND EVALUATIONS OF IW PROGRAMS

At present, there is no comprehensive audit of the vulnerabilities, technical performance, or management efforts of most federal departments and agencies. Experts do feel that the agencies in the national security effort make a notably better effort than most civil agencies to conduct such evaluations, and to establish controls like "red teams" that can test the actual performance capability of federal efforts. They indicate that NSA also is much more capable of using its technical expertise to push management toward ensuring the proper level of technical expertise and competence than NIST, in large part because NIST lacks the authority and visibility to be effective.

Experts have identified a number of additional problems:

- *There is a basic imbalance in the approach to technology, particularly in civil agencies.* Present policy guidance and review focuses almost exclusively on prevention rather than remediation. There are few incentives to create an effective capability to cope with a successful attack, or to ensure that equipment and architecture are chosen to resist attack. Patches and fixes are used to try to defend, rather than create robust and recoverable systems.

- *The federal government is not organized to develop quick updates and patches.* Federal agencies are extremely slow to update their protection systems and software. Updates and patches can be installed six months to nine months after they become available, leaving given systems vulnerable far longer than should be the case. For security and other reasons, there is no use of automated patches, with some secure access and acceptance process.

- *There is no ongoing federal-wide warning and technology review process.* There is no central management of technology review or net technical assessment process to keep all managers and CIOs informed, particularly at the unclassified level. Audits do not evaluate whether personnel are adequate, future technical risk, or whether spending is adequate to allow an agency to meet federal guidelines.

- *The use of outsourcing for systems, system components, and even protection systems creates major risks that cannot be appraised until an attack occurs.* In many cases, no effort is made to ensure that the purchase of goods and services does not involve foreign companies or key foreign personnel in U.S. companies. In one case, the FAA subcontracted critical air control subsystems to a firm staffed largely by Chinese nationals.

Chapter 6

Role of State and Local Governments

It is obvious that state and local governments confront many of the same problems and issues as the federal government. What is not obvious is the level of progress that is being made in law enforcement, self-defense, and counterattack capability, and what standards should really be applied.

It is also not at all apparent that clear demarcations of responsibility exist to make state and local authorities fully aware of the limits that they can expect in outside aid, and their responsibility in communicating data on attacks and law enforcement intelligence. It is all very well to talk about partnership, but successful partnership is based as much on the clear demarcation of responsibility as on cooperation.

In general, however, there seems to be a consensus at all levels of government that state and local governments generally are not organized effectively to deal with the changes in critical infrastructure and information technology. Many programs at this level, when they exist, are badly underfunded and lag badly behind the private sector. This is systemic in many areas of protection capability; at the prevention, mitigation, and reconstitution levels.

If the federal government needs auditing and effectiveness measures, so do state and local governments. There need to be clear standards in law and regulation that enforce effective action, and some form of reporting that ensures that the success of state and local action can be monitored by the citizens of given communities and states. At the same time, the federal government needs to assess critical national vulnerabilities and defense capabilities by state and community. That said, it is unclear that the federal government has standards that support adequate assessment of state and local vulnerability and prevention, mitigation, and reconstitution capabilities, or can provide the kind of guidance that would allow state and local governments to perform such analysis.

Chapter 7

Role of Private Industry

Government is naturally obsessed with itself. The vast majority of critical systems, however, are in the private and civil sectors. Moreover, the technology, software, and information systems used by individual elements of the private and civil sectors are evolving so rapidly and are so specialized that there are severe limits to what government can do to provide day-to-day protection. To put it bluntly, roughly 90 percent of the burden of defense must fall on the user, and the same is true of nearly 100 percent of the burden of day-to-day defense against cyber-crime and hackers.

Many entities already understand this. They are under constant attack, and many of them deploy relatively sophisticated defenses in response. Many, however, do not or have not yet realized the sheer scale of the steadily growing problem they face. Some internalize the problem, concealing losses from law enforcement agencies because of the fear of appearing vulnerable. Others may be under the illusion that a combination of federal action and law enforcement activity can offer more protection than is really feasible. The fact is that any "partnership" between the federal government and the private sector will be acutely limited.

There also are many parts of the private and civil sectors that take a stove-pipe approach to vulnerability and do not consider the impact they have on other elements of the private sector or their full range of vulnerability. Many entities underfund all defense and reconstitution activity because there is insufficient pressure to interfere with efforts to minimize expenses, and there are inadequate liability, insurance, and auditing standards to force affective action. Liability laws have not yet been applied or are unclear as to the failure to develop adequate protection and reconstitution capabilities. The "reasonableness" standard for performance is so low that it has little practical effect. Many companies have the same problems in dealing with their CIP office as agencies in the federal government.

Like the federal government, there is far more emphasis on prevention than mitigation and recovery capability. Even in these areas, however, many experts estimate that corporations are spending only about one-third of what they should, and both CEOs and CFOs are often more a barrier to effective action than they are advocates.

There is also a fear of the costs of disclosure and cooperation. The laws relating to FOIA present the problem that reporting to the government can become public and used to discover vulnerabilities. Proprietary actions can be compromised, and reports of successful attacks can damage a company's reputation and stock value.

One key implication of these realities is that the private sector must formally assume this responsibility: The present legal requirements for private and civil sector entities to take full action to defend their information and computer systems, and other parts of the nation's critical infrastructure, remains somewhat ambiguous. The legal penalties, and civil and criminal liability for failing to take effective action is poorly defined and does not create the kind of pressure for such action created by other bodies of law and regulation. There are no requirements that force disclosure in a prospectus of successful attacks, the failure of defense, the annual level of corporate action, or vulnerability and protective efforts. These rules are clearly defined with regard to medical records and some aspects of legal practice, and the penalties are often severe. Clear requirements and liabilities must be established for all aspects of government, commericial, and NGO activities.

Changes may well be needed in legal liability and criminal law relating to critical infrastructure protection. There is a need to review the present legal penalties and liabilities for actual violators as well. While the result varies by case, current precedents and penalties seem to understate the seriousness of cyber-crime and attacks. Similarly, the due diligence aspects of insurance coverage may need review to ensure that insurance companies only provide coverage to firms that take effective cyber-defense measures, and coverage is invalidated when companies do not make a suitable effort to maintain and improve their defenses.

Equally important, state and local governments and all elements of the private sector—businesses, utilities, and NGOs—need to explicitly assume responsibility for the vulnerability of their systems and activities. Furthermore, they bear responsibility for having the ability to respond to attacks both during and after the attack, the ability to ameliorate attacks, and the ability to reconstitute their capabilities and/or provide alternative back-up systems.

It cannot be emphasized too firmly that any regulations and laws, insurance requirements, and internal efforts that focus only on cyber-defense are so inherently flawed as to be as much a source of future problems as a solution. Pushing the private sector toward more effective defense must be based on pushing it toward the most cost-effective mix of solutions, and not simply toward active cyber-defense.

One key aspect of such activity is to define what information systems must be isolated from the Internet and outside access, given rapid recovery capability, and be supported by back-up systems or emergency alternatives. The survival or collapse of well over 90 percent of the nations commercial (and probably governmental) information systems may create serious temporary problems and/or even bankrupt any given firm. Such problems do not merit federal help and have no national importance. The government does not owe any private entity protection beyond routine law enforcement effort, and their survival is unimportant to homeland defense. In fact, the collapse or destruction of companies and NGOs that fail to take effective self-protection measures may ultimately be a key factor forcing others to improve.

It is the relative handful of truly critical systems that really require full protection, and cyber-defense must clearly identify such systems and give them the protection they need.

Chapter 8

Lessons from Other Nations: International Vulnerability

All nations face roughly the same basic problems as the U.S. Most developed nations, and an increasing number of developing nations, face the same problems with cyber-crime and hacking, and many are the subject of ideological attacks on their information systems and vulnerable to cyber-war. Nations like Kosovo have already shown that attacks by state actors are a reality of modern war, and potential threats like China, Russia, and Iran have a well-developed literature on cyber-warfare, and a growing technical base for conducting such attacks.

At present, international law is inadequate to deal with cyber-crime. A recent survey conducted by McConnell International showed that Albania, Australia, Brazil, Bulgaria, Burundi, Canada, Chile, China, Cuba, Czech Republic, Denmark, Dominican Republic, Egypt, Estonia, Ethiopia, Fiji, France, Gambia, Hungary, Iceland, India, Iran, Italy, Japan, Jordan, Kazakhstan, Latvia, Lebanon, Lesotho, Malaysia, Malta, Mauritius, Moldova, Morocco, New Zealand, Nicaragua, Nigeria, Norway, Peru, Philippines, Poland, Romania, South Africa, Spain, Sudan, Turkey, United Kingdom, United States, Vietnam, Yugoslavia, Zambia, and Zimbabwe supported the conclusions that most existing laws in these countries failed to effectively deter cyber-crime, although no assessment was made of overall cyber-vulnerability, and the capability to defend or respond in cyber-war.[122]

This survey was started when the Philippines found its laws inadequate to sustain charges against the alleged perpetrator of the "Love

Bug" virus that jammed electronic mail networks in May 2000. It found that 33 of the 52 nations surveyed had not updated their criminal codes to deal with any offense tied to the use of computers. Ten of the countries surveyed enacted laws to address five or fewer of the ten types of offenses at issue, while nine said they were prepared to prosecute six types of offenses or more. The survey showed that U.S. laws covered nine of the ten crimes. Only the Philippines, where the "Love Bug" virus originated, had enacted laws to cover all ten types of crimes. The offenses included data-related crimes including interception, modification, and theft; network tampering, including interference and sabotage; "crimes of access" including hacking and virus distribution; and computer-associated crimes such as aiding and abetting cyber-criminals, computer fraud, and computer forgery.

The U.S. worked with NATO and the EU to try to create standards and agreements for cyber-defense; and many allied nations, such as Canada, are now exploring many of the same issues as the U.S. Real progress may be imminent in dealing with cyber-crime. The U.S. endorsed most of a proposed cyber-crime pact drafted by the 41-nation Council of Europe in December 2000. The Council of Europe first released this draft of the Convention on Cyber-Crime on April 27, 2000. It is the first multilateral instrument drafted to address the problems posed by the spread of criminal activity on computer networks.[123] The U.S. had participated in the drafting of the Council of Europe Convention for nearly two years. The convention will be finalized by the Steering Committee on European Crime Problems, and be submitted to the Committee of Ministers for adoption before it is opened to members of the Council of Europe and observer nations—including the U.S.—for signature.

The text of the draft convention has the following key provisions affecting each nation that agrees to it:

- Each Party shall adopt such legislative and other measures as may be necessary to establish as criminal offences under its domestic law when committed intentionally 3 the access 4 to the whole or any part of a computer system without right 5. A Party may require that the offence be committed either by infringing security measures or with the intent of obtaining computer data or other dishonest intent 6, or in relation to a computer system that is connected to another computer system.

- Each Party shall adopt such legislative and other measures as may be necessary to establish as criminal offences under its domestic law when committed intentionally the interception without right, made by technical means, of non-public 7 transmissions of computer data to, from or within a computer system, including electromagnetic emissions from a computer system carrying such computer data. A Party may require that the offence be committed with dishonest intent, or in relation to a computer system that is connected to another computer system.

- Each Party shall adopt such legislative and other measures as may be necessary to establish as criminal offences under its domestic law when committed intentionally the damaging, deletion, deterioration, alteration 8 or suppression 9 of computer data without right.

- Each Party shall adopt such legislative and other measures as may be necessary to establish as criminal offences under its domestic law when committed intentionally the serious hindering without right of the functioning of a computer system by inputting, transmitting, damaging, deleting, deteriorating, altering or suppressing computer data.

- Each Party shall adopt such legislative and other measures as may be necessary to establish as criminal offences under its domestic law when committed intentionally and without right:

  - the production, sale, procurement for use, import, distribution or otherwise making available of: a device, including a computer program, designed or adapted primarily for the purpose of committing any of the offences established in accordance with Articles 2–5;

  - a computer password, access code, or similar data by which the whole or any part of a computer system is capable of being accessed with intent that it be used for the purpose of committing the offences established in Articles 2–5; and

  - the possession of an item with intent that it be used for the purpose of committing the offenses established in Articles 2–5. A Party may require by law that a number of such items be possessed before criminal liability attaches.

- Each Party shall adopt such legislative and other measures as may be necessary to establish as criminal offences under its domestic law when committed intentionally and without right the input, alteration, deletion, or suppression of computer data, resulting in inauthentic data with the intent that it be considered or acted upon for legal purposes as if it were authentic 10, regardless whether or not the data is directly readable and intelligible. A Party may require an intent to defraud, or similar dishonest intent, before criminal liability attaches.

- Each Party shall adopt such legislative and other measures as may be necessary to establish as criminal offences under its domestic law, when committed intentionally and without right, the causing of a loss of property to another by: any input, alteration, deletion or suppression of computer data, and/or any interference with the functioning of a computer or system, with the intent of procuring, without right, an economic benefit for oneself or for another.

- Each Party shall adopt such legislative and other measures as may be necessary to establish as criminal offences under its domestic law when committed intentionally and without right to include the following conduct: offering or making available child pornography through a computer system; distributing or transmitting child pornography through a computer system; producing child pornography for the purpose of its distribution through a computer system; procuring child pornography through a computer system for oneself or for another; possessing child pornography in a computer system or on a computer-data storage medium.

- Each Party shall adopt such legislative and other measures as may be necessary to establish as criminal offences under its domestic law the infringement of copyright, as defined under the law of that Party pursuant to the obligations it has undertaken under the Paris Act of 24 July 1971 of the Berne Convention for the Protection of Literary and Artistic Works the Agreement on Trade-Related Aspects of Intellectual Property Rights and the WIPO Copyright Treaty, with the exception of any moral rights conferred by such Conventions, where such acts are committed intentionally, on a commercial scale and by means of a computer system.

- Each Party shall adopt such legislative and other measures as may be necessary to establish as criminal offences under its domestic law the infringement of related rights, as defined under the law of that Party pursuant to the obligations it has undertaken under the International Convention for the Protection of Performers, Producers of Phonograms and Broadcasting Organizations done in Rome (Rome Convention), the Agreement on Trade-Related Aspects of Intellectual Property Rights and the WIPO Performances and Phonograms Treaty, with the exception of any moral rights conferred by such Conventions, where such acts are committed intentionally, on a commercial scale and by means of a computer system.

- Each Party shall adopt such legislative and other measures as may be necessary to ensure that a legal person can be held liable for the criminal offences established in accordance with this Convention, committed for its benefit by any natural person, acting either individually or as part of an organ of the legal person, who has a leading position within the legal person, based on: a power of representation of the legal person; an authority to take decisions on behalf of the legal person; or an authority to exercise control within the legal person.

- Each Party shall take the necessary measures to ensure that a legal person can be held liable where the lack of supervision or control by a natural person referred to in paragraph 1 has made possible the commission of a criminal offences established in accordance with this Convention for the benefit of that legal person by a natural person under its authority.

- Each Party shall adopt such legislative and other measures as may be necessary to enable its competent authorities, in connection with a specific criminal matter, to order or similarly obtain the expeditious preservation of data that has been stored by means of a computer system, in particular where there are grounds to believe that the data is particularly vulnerable 2 to loss or modification.

- Each Party shall adopt such legislative or other measures as may be necessary to oblige the custodian or other person who is to preserve the data to keep confidential the undertaking of such procedures for the period of time provided for by its domestic law.

- Each Party shall adopt such legislative or other measures as may be necessary to: ensure the expeditious preservation of that traffic data regardless whether one or more service providers were involved in the transmission of that communication; and ensure the expeditious disclosure to the Party's competent authority, or a person designated by that authority, of a sufficient amount of traffic data in order

- Each Party shall adopt such legislative and other measures as may be necessary to empower its competent authorities, for the purposes of criminal investigations or proceedings, to search or similarly access:

  - a computer system or part of it and computer data stored therein; and

  - a computer-data storage medium in which computer data may be stored, in its territory.

- Each Party shall adopt such legislative and other measures as may be necessary to ensure that where its authorities search or similarly access a specific computer system or part of it, using the measures referred to in paragraph 1 (a), and have grounds to believe that the data sought is stored in another computer system or part of it in its territory, and such data is lawfully accessible from or available to the initial system, such authorities shall be able to expeditiously extend the search or similar accessing to the other system.

- Each Party shall adopt such legislative and other measures as may be necessary to empower its competent authorities, for the purposes of criminal investigations or proceedings, to seize or similarly secure computer data.

- Each Party shall adopt such legislative and other measures as may be necessary to empower its competent authorities to order for the purposes of criminal investigations or proceedings any person who has knowledge about the functioning of the computer system or measures applied to protect the computer data therein to provide all necessary information, as is reasonable, to enable the undertaking of the measures referred to in paragraphs 1 and 2.

- Each Party shall adopt such legislative and other measures as may be necessary to empower, for the purpose of criminal investigations or proceedings, its competent authorities to:

  - collect or record through application of technical means on the territory of that Party, and

- compel a service provider, within its technical ability, to collect or record through application of technical means on the territory of that Party, or co-operate and assist the competent authorities in the collection or recording of, traffic data, in real-time, associated with specified communications in its territory transmitted by means of a computer system.

- Each Party shall adopt such legislative and other measures as may be necessary, for the purpose of criminal investigations or proceedings related to the range of serious offences to be determined by domestic law, to empower its competent authorities to:

  - collect or record through application of technical means on the territory of that Party, and

  - compel a service provider, within its technical ability, to collect or record through application of technical means on the territory of that Party, or co-operate and assist the competent authorities in the collection or recording of, content data, in real-time, of specified communications in its territory transmitted by means of a computer system.

- Each Party shall adopt such legislative and other measures as may be necessary to oblige a service provider to keep confidential the fact of and any information about the execution of any power provided for under Articles 20 and

- Each Party shall adopt such legislative and other measures as may be necessary to establish jurisdiction over any offence established in accordance with Articles 2–11 of this Convention, when the offence is committed in its territory; or on board a ship flying the flag or registered under the laws of that Party; or on board an aircraft registered under the laws of that Party; or by one of its nationals, if the offence is punishable under criminal law where it was committed or if the offence is committed outside the territorial jurisdiction of any State.

- The Parties shall co-operate with each other, in accordance with the provisions of this chapter, and through application of relevant international instruments on international co-operation in criminal matters, arrangements agreed on the basis of uniform or reciprocal legislation, and domestic laws, to the widest extent possible for the purposes of investigations or proceedings concerning criminal offences related to computer systems and data, or for the collection of electronic evidence of a criminal offence.

- This article applies to extradition between Parties for the criminal offences established in accordance with Articles 2–11 of this Convention, provided that they are punishable under the laws of both Parties concerned by deprivation of liberty for a maximum period of at least one year, or by a more severe penalty. Where an extradition treaty or reciprocal arrangement legislation is in force between two or more Parties, which requires a different minimum penalty for extradition, the minimum penalty provided for in such treaty or reciprocal arrangement shall instead apply.

- The Parties shall afford one another mutual assistance to the widest extent possible for the purpose of investigations or proceedings concerning criminal offences related to computer systems and data, or for the collection of electronic evidence of a criminal offence.

- Each Party shall designate a central authority or authorities that shall be responsible for sending and answering requests for mutual assistance, the execution of such requests, or the transmission of them to the authorities competent for their execution. The central authorities shall communicate directly with each other.

- A Party may, within the limits of its domestic law, without prior request, forward to another Party information obtained within the framework of its own investigations when it considers that the disclosure of such information might assist the receiving Party in initiating or carrying out investigations or proceedings concerning criminal offences established in accordance with this Convention or might lead to a request for cooperation by that Party under this chapter.

- A Party may request another Party to order or otherwise obtain the expeditious preservation of data stored by means of a computer system, which is located within the territory of that other Party and in respect of which the requesting Party intends to submit a request for mutual assistance for the search or similar access, seizure or similar securing, or disclosure of the data.

- Upon receiving the request from another Party, the requested Party shall take all appropriate measures to preserve expeditiously the specified data in accordance with its domestic law. For the purposes of responding to a request, dual criminality shall not be required as a condition to providing such preservation, but may be required as a condition for the disclosure of the data to the requesting Party.

- A Party may request another Party to search or similarly access, seize or similarly secure, and disclose data stored by means of a computer system located within the territory of the requested Party, including data that has been preserved pursuant to Article 29.

- A Party may, without obtaining the authorization of another Party: access publicly available (open source) stored computer data, regardless of where the data is located geographically; or access or receive, through a computer system in its territory, stored computer data located in another Party, if the Party obtains the lawful and voluntary consent of the person who has the lawful authority to disclose the data to the Party through that computer system.

- The Parties shall provide mutual assistance to each other with respect to the real-time collection of traffic data associated with specified communications in its territory transmitted by means of a computer system. Subject to paragraph 2, assistance shall be governed by the conditions and procedures provided for under domestic law.

- Each Party shall designate a point of contact available on a 24 hour, 7 day per week basis in order to ensure the provision of immediate assistance for the purpose of the investigation of criminal offenses related to the use of computer systems and data, or for the collection of electronic evidence of any criminal offense.

Other countries outside Europe are also deeply involved in dealing with such criminal and lower-level threats. China, India, and Israel are just a few of the nations outside the West that play a growing role in the development of advanced commercial systems. The accession of all countries to the Convention on Cyber-Crime will be critical to creating an effective body of law. Broad accession will be critical to international cooperation in law enforcement and to the modernization of coordinating groups like Interpol.

The Convention on Cyber-Crime does not, however, create any common standards for dealing with cyber-war, and large-scale asymmetric attacks by states, their proxies, or the kind of well-organized terrorist group that could emerge in the future. All countries keep their capabilities for cyber-warfare highly classified, although it is clear that every Western state, Russia, China, and Israel have highly developed capabilities, and many other states are seeking to acquire them or may have important elements of such capabilities.

As yet, the open literature does not provide an adequate basis for either determining what we can learn from our allies, just how serious the threat from potential opponents is and will become, or what basis exists for cooperation with our allies and within critical bodies like NATO. There is a clear need to begin to survey allied policies and actions and to develop a cooperative approach wherever possible, particularly because this will be critical to joint action in the event of major attacks, because of the international nature of many key information systems and financial networks, and because of the multinational nature of many key corporate targets.

One potentially critical area of vulnerability is international organizations and NGOs. There does not seem to be any clear assessment of the efforts of organizations like the World Bank, IMF, United Nations, and Red Cross. The cyber-defense of international bodies and NGOs needs detailed examination.

The growth of multinationals and mergers presents another problem. There are no common laws and regulations that require adequate efforts by foreign-based firms or which apply to all elements of U.S.–based multinationals. It is unclear what efforts multinationals are making to reduce insider threats and attacks, and limit the dispersion of knowledge of their protection systems and vulnerabilities to a wide range of foreign nationals and countries—a problem compounded by the extensive use of outsourcing. The U.S. must act to ensure that foreign companies operating in the U.S., and those aspects of multinationals operating outside the U.S., but still under some areas of U.S. jurisdiction, take the same cyber-defense measures as U.S. domestic companies.

Chapter 9

Conclusions and Recommendations

There are obvious problems in making detailed recommendations about the U.S. government role in critical infrastructure protection in general, and in dealing with the threats posed by cyber-warfare and cyber-terrorism in particular. It is clear that the U.S. has made substantial progress in defining policies and strategies for dealing with the new threats to its critical infrastructure. It is also clear that there are a wide range of new federal programs that are both improving federal capabilities, and developing the ability of the federal government to work with state and local governments and with the private and civil sectors.

At the same time, there is a disturbing gap between the military focus on asymmetric warfare and the civil focus on cyber-crime and cyber-terrorism. There is a flood of uncertain and poorly defined data on the threat, much of which is highly anecdotal. Incidents tend to be exaggerated while the overall pattern in the threat may be understated or missed altogether. Cost and risk estimates are issued that are little more than guesstimates, often using dubious methods and data. There is a critical lack of technological net assessment of the trends in offense and defense, and of the relative capabilities of governments and the private sector.

Civil federal programs lack transparency, and many seem to lack effective management in the sense that there is no clear program rationale. There are no detailed threat assessments, program budget and future-year plans, or well-defined future milestones and measures of effectiveness. National security programs reflect the same lack of transparency, and added layers of security concerns make it substantially harder to assess them than civil programs.

There is also much the same dichotomy in federal critical infrastructure programs as there is in federal efforts to deal with counterterrorism and the CBRN threat. It is not clear what level of threat the U.S. is really planning to deal with, whether it is seriously planning for major cyber-warfare and cyber-terrorist attacks. At the policy level, it gives the impression that it is. At the practical level, its activity seems to be concentrated on lower levels of attack, which are more the province of law enforcement.

Accordingly, the U.S. should consider the following recommendations for homeland defense:

- *The U.S. government must establish a clear distinction between general cyber-crime and cyber-warfare, and tailor the federal role and response accordingly.* The U.S. faces an inevitable ongoing and growing problem with cyber-crime and low-level cyber-attacks with motivations ranging from treating hacking as a sport to employee sabotage and ideologically driven terrorism. Unlike the normal range of similar threats to the nation's physical infrastructure, these can be expected to grow in at least the same proportion as dependence on computers, information systems, and electronic commerce.

  Cyber-warfare falls under the obvious authority of the national security apparatus, whereas cyber-crime is a law enforcement problem. Both however, have a strong private sector component. While the federal government cannot ignore some law enforcement responsibility in dealing with such threats, it is clear that virtually all of the burden of defense must fall on individual users in the private and civil sectors, and in state and local governments. There is no practical way that the federal government will ever develop the technical skills, and overcome its lack of specialized competence in ways that enable it to defend the vast majority of physical nodes in America's critical infrastructure or critical e-commerce, computer, and information systems. In fact, at least 90% of the burden of day-to-day defense must fall on the private user or corporation.

  Where the federal government does have an important role to play is in the area of national security. This includes protection from any form of sabotage or exploitation of systems or data that is key to the well-being of the nation.

  There now seems to be a clear disconnect between the efforts in the U.S. to plan offensive cyber-warfare and efforts at cyber-defense. Many defenders also assert that "Technology 101" favors the attacker, prevents attribution, and makes counteroffense difficult or impossible. Some "attackers" and intelligence experts sharply question these views, and others see offense and defense as an ongoing duel whose outcome is unclear. Either way, escalation of capabilities is inevitable on both sides. The key to success in protecting information infrastructure will be to keep pace with developments on both sides of the equation, and then to develop battlefield dominance capability in the same manner as we approach issues like air superiority and C⁴I for battlefield picture.

U.S. military and defense officials involved in information warfare and planning and executing cyber-war have divided views. Those directly involved in cyber-offense, however, generally seem to feel that carrying out a successful major cyber-attack is far more difficult than those outside the national security arena recognize. They do not minimize the risk of cyber-attacks, but they feel they will have limited impact and that many if not most critical systems are isolated, difficult to identify and enter in concerted attacks, and can be reconstituted within an acceptable timeframe and cost.

There is a clear need for some form of annual net technical assessment of the balance of offense and defense that can guide federal programs, and whose conclusions can be used to advise government, business, and NGOs. Much of this work will involve some of the most sensitive areas of classified operations and technology in the U.S. government, and such a net assessment virtually has to be conducted within the national security community. At the same time, ways must be found to convincingly communicate the results to other federal government agencies, state and local governments, and to the private sector. There is also a clear need for ongoing outside debate about the balance between offensive and defense, and to move beyond poorly supported assertions that can either over or understate the threat.

• *The U.S. needs to determine what its real vulnerabilities are, and what action is needed to deter attacks, provide defense, and to respond.* Homeland defense does not consist of expanding the federal role in critical infrastructure protection at random—an effort that may well prove counterproductive by creating false priorities and promising capabilities the government cannot deliver. Homeland defense does, however, consist of clearly identifying critical vulnerabilities and taking well-focused and prudent federal action. At present, there seems to be little coherent vulnerability analysis, little prioritization, and little effort to distinguish what level of federal role is really involved.

Serious problems also exist over how to estimate vulnerability, risk, and cost. Most of the estimates of the cost of cyber-crime and cracking, and the economic risk of cyber-attacks, seem to be little more than crude back of the envelope calculations with little or no credibility. Many, if not most, seem designed to grossly exaggerate the risk and cost to make a point.

These problems are compounded by the tendency to ignore the fact that ordinary crime and systems failures are an endemic reality in every aspect of government, business, and the nation's infrastructure. Storms, weather patterns, mechanical failures and a host of other actuarial realities constantly "attack" the nation's critical infrastructure and the normal operations of government and business. Many of these events also lead to exaggerated estimates of loss and cost, which ignore the ability to recoup any losses over time.

There are major problems in identifying the point at which any successful attack would, in fact, be serious enough to justify federal intervention or really damage the nation's critical infrastructure in serious and lasting ways. From the perspective of any given business or NGO, a catastrophic attack on its information systems could be crippling or have massive consequences. However, from a national perspective, businesses and NGOs fail or suffer crippling damage for many reasons, and the nation has survived. Major temporary failures in the operation of communications systems, commerce, utility services, stock transactions, etc. are an ongoing fact of life.

At the same time, the pressure to create steadily more complex systems can create chains of interlocking vulnerability that are very difficult to detect and predict. It can be argued that many who assess cyber-vulnerability fail to evaluate the ongoing evolution of defensive efforts in reaction to the constant pressure from crackers and cyber-criminals. Yet, it also can be argued that models do not exist for analyzing complex patterns of vulnerability to more sophisticated patterns of attack. The limited number of federal tests and exercises that have attempted to measure vulnerability to date raise real questions about such vulnerabilities, although some suffer from a structure that exercises technical assumptions rather than measures actually vulnerability.

This again creates a need for an annual net technical assessment to establish the actual state of vulnerability in government and the private sector, and the areas where federal intervention may really be justified in terms of homeland defense. This will present major technical challenges, but at present there seems to be no real basis for prioritizing federal efforts or guiding state and local governments and the private sector.

The lack of such vulnerability assessments also tends to favor those who believe in boosting defense against ongoing or known methods of cyber-attack rather than solutions based on designing less vulnerable systems and increasing isolation from attack. Sufficient needs to be put into adding measures to reconstitute systems, provide less capable back-up systems and alternatives, and ameliorate attacks or failures once they occur. Specifically addressing all of these options should be a critical aspect of such a vulnerability assessment.

- *Establish ongoing technological net assessments.* Technology is changing very rapidly, resulting in constant shifts in the balance of offensive and defensive technology such that the federal government cannot rely on impressionistic or anecdotal studies, law enforcement statistics, or the technological forecasting of program advocates. Thus, every federal agency needs to carry out a detailed technological net assessment that should be reviewed by independent bodies with the proper technical competence, such as the Office of Net Assessment in the Department of Defense. Such technical net assessment evaluations including countermeasure and cost-to-defeat analysis of all proposed new activities and all RDT&E and procurement programs are also needed in supporting budget and program reviews of related programs conducted by the GAO, CBO, and OMB. The evaluation should also be required in agency and individual program justifications.

- *Define the national governmental and private systems that are truly critical and ensure they are isolated from attack, emergency alternatives exist, and they can be rapidly reconstituted.* Information systems will remain a curse as well as a blessing, unless the U.S. clearly identifies the systems that are truly critical to the functions of its government, its economy, its defense, its law enforcement, and the well-being of its citizens and requires that they have suitable protection. Many such systems are already isolated from the Internet, and require special care in terms of access, clearance of personnel, and other protective measures. This cannot be left to ad hoc efforts, however, and damage to a relatively limited number of systems with such importance is far more important than the result of hacking, cracking, cyber-crime, or cyber-terrorism in the overwhelming majority of systems. All systems are created grossly unequal in importance and vulnerability, and homeland defense must be based on this fact.

- *The federal government needs to decide at what point federal intervention is required.* What is the level of organized foreign, terrorist, or extremist attack that individual users cannot be expected to defend against. This level of cyber-attack requires major federal action to deter and defend. The second is a type of attack which goes beyond a limited threat that might temporarily cripple a given node in the nation's infrastructure, or an important target like one of the nation's major corporations. This would be an attack that would threaten a key portion of the nation's infrastructure, a key function of government, or the health of any sector in the nation's economy.

- *There is a need for central federal coordination and review of a strategy, future year plan, program budget, and annual budget, and for a regular annual cycle of such activity.* There is broad agreement that some central office is needed to coordinate the federal effort, to ensure proper auditing and capability, and to coordinate emergency response capability. Such a coordinator needs sufficient rank and authority to speak for the President on these issues, and to ensure that agency budget submissions include adequate programs and funding. Some have proposed an independent office similar to the Y2K program, some a new form of drug czar, and some a cabinet level officer. Similar arguments are being made about providing a coordinator to deal with weapons of mass destruction attacks and all of homeland defense. These issues, however, need far more careful study. Thus, a Presidential Task Force should be set up to review the broad need to deal with all of the emerging threats to the American homeland, and to draft recommendations and a PDD for the next president.

- *Independent audits of federal vulnerability and competence in critical infrastructure protection should be carried out regularly.* There is no more reason to assume that federal entities will take proper responsibility for critical infrastructure protection than to assume that they can be trusted to control the efficiency of their accounting and audit procedures. Moreover, the pace of technology change is so rapid, that it is not reasonable to assume that most departments and agencies can develop the necessary competence to assess every aspect of their vulnerability. Therefore, there is a need to either charge the GAO or an independent office with annual audits of all federal agencies and departments to ensure adequate federal efforts in the protection of the nations critical infrastructure and federal computer/information systems. It should also be clear that the secretary or head of a department or agency will have personal responsibility for the department's performance. Also, in order to avoid the present practice of assigning the CIO tasks without adequate management support or funding the chief financial officer should be made to share equal responsibility with the chief information officer.

- *There needs to be an understanding that defense also involves offense.* As yet, the U.S. government has not created a credible process for "active defense" against foreign attacks. During Kosovo the U.S. clearly demonstrated that it was not ready for either defensive or offensive cyber-warfare and would be vulnerable to large-scale cyber-terrorism. It has not come to grips with the issue of whether it should create a process of deterrence based on the near-certain threat of retaliation and use of the offensive. Regardless of U.S. rhetoric about information warfare, its practice focuses on defense. Indeed, the U.S. government risks becoming tied down in legalistic barriers and procedures at a time when it is, and is likely to remain, the nation most vulnerable to cyber-warfare. Indeed, the need for a clear doctrine and basis in law for active defense, cyber-warfare, cyber-deterrence and cyber-retaliation is a critical priority.

- *It is unclear whether the tools for offensive online warfare exist, and extensive research and development efforts may be needed to improve them.* A doctrine for usage is also needed, although the Department of Defense's general counsel did release an "Assessment of International Legal Issues in Information Operations" in May 1999. Many potential adversaries—including those actively involved in attacks directed at the U.S. at the present time have put such a doctrine in place (Russia, China, etc.).

- *There must be a clear central organization in the Department of Defense that is trained and equipped to fight cyber-warfare and respond to large-scale foreign attacks by governments, terrorists, and extremists.* This center must be prepared to conduct such operations in the context of broader economic warfare, conventional warfare, or in parallel with covert or terrorist attacks using large-scale explosive devices, selectively attacking the physical elements in our infrastructure, or using chemical, biological, radiological, or nuclear weapons. The Department of Defense tends to talk a fight it cannot execute, and to compartment its response to different kinds of regular and asymmetric warfare. There must be a clear central point for conducting cyber-defense and cyber-warfare with close ties to a similar center of excellence in the intelligence community. It must be given suitable funding and equipment, and be supported by similar centers of excellence in each military service and unified and specified command. It must be clearly linked to a similar center for conducting cyber-defense and cyber-warfare in the federal law enforcement community. There must also be clear procedures through which the Department of Defense can assist federal, state, and local authorities. It is easy to assign responsibility, but the issue is to create effective capability.

- *The U.S. government needs to develop a clear response doctrine.* The U.S. military has a clear responsibility to conduct information warfare against a military opponent. It is not clear who has a responsibility to conduct offensive cyber-warfare against a major terrorist threat, or what level of attack the U.S. must be ready to conduct against an opponent's government, media, economy, and civil services. It is not even clear what level of action can be taken before it is considered an act of war. As long as cyber-attacks remain limited and little more than an irritant from a broad national perspective, this may not be a critical issue. The U.S. should at least consider whether it should develop a deterrent capability for massive retaliation that could convincingly devastate the information and communication systems of any opponent, cripple its economy, and produce direct and indirect casualties far higher than any opponent can inflict upon the U.S. This should include a *very* rapid chain of command for response. Response times are incredibly important in this arena, and multiple layers of approval will fatally compromise any action by adding excessive latency. A standardized reporting distribution channel and event report format (with attached response authorization request) might be a good idea.

- *The U.S. must define the nature of "cyber-neutrality" and "cyber-collateral damage."* The U.S. cannot allow constraints to be placed on effective retaliatory and offensive cyber-warfare without carefully considering the nature of the future battles it may have to fight. There already are efforts to define the scope of the Geneva Convention in ways that would effective preclude states like the U.S. from taking effective offensive and retaliatory action while, at the same time, allowing more radical governments to hide under the shield of such legal doctrine, or to use proxies. The responsibility of states to prevent the use of their facilities as transit routes for cyber-attacks is unclear, as are their rights as "neutrals." The same is true of the responsibility of host and transit states to block terrorist and extremist action from their territory.

- *The U.S. should reserve the right to respond unilaterally to attacks against its infrastructure.* To avoid any political problem that might arise as a result of the damage done to the infrastructure of neutral countries through which attacks take place, the U.S. should state as a matter of policy that poor defense on the part of other governments makes them de facto contributors to the attack against the U.S., and thus abrogates virtually any responsibility on the part of the U.S. to limit response channels only to the original source. This then also partially mitigates the problems of attribution since the original source of the attack can almost never be known for certain, and makes every transit country recognize its responsibility in protecting information infrastructure as part of the global economy.

- *Existing conventions and agreements on international law, terrorism, and the laws of war need to be changed to reflect the reality of cyber-threats and cyber-warfare.* The present body of law and international agreements was never designed to deal with the risk of large-scale cyber-crime and cyber-warfare, any more than it was designed to deal with the risks of large-scale chemical, biological, radiological, or nuclear covert, terrorist, and extremist attacks. Some basic agreements, like the Geneva Convention, can be interpreted in ways that prevent effective retaliation and defense, and as forcing the U.S. to rely largely on passive defenses at the point of attack. A comprehensive review is needed of the current body of international law, and some form of new convention and series of legal agreements may be needed so that the U.S., its allies, and other moderate and law abiding states can cooperate effectively in the defense of their respective homelands and counterattack under clearly understood conditions that will act as an effective deterrent.

- *The U.S. needs to determine agency responsibility for major levels of cyber-attack, and create supporting legislation.* At the point where cyber-warfare or cyber-terrorism/extremism seriously threatens the national interest, the U.S. must be prepared to respond as if it were dealing with any other act of war. This means taking coherent federal offensive and defensive action, possibly as part of a broader ongoing conflict. In practice, foreign attacks are likely to mean a transition from responsibility by domestic agencies to responsibility by the Department of Defense.

- *The U.S. must redefine the role of its intelligence community and develop the proper technical expertise.* So far, the nation's intelligence systems have not resolved the issue of how to conduct information warfare without seriously compromising their collection and analytic capabilities. More broadly, it is not clear what roles CIA and NSA are to play in critical infrastructure protection, and how well they are developing the necessary technical capabilities. A number of outside experts serious question whether NSA is modernizing its roles and missions to look at a different electronic future, or whether the intelligence community can attract and retain the necessary technically skilled personnel. One critical issue is the extent to which national security requires an approach to intelligence and critical infrastructure that goes beyond the previous definition of national security and gives new priority to economic and cyber-warfare and other attacks on the U.S. homeland that do not involve conventional acts of war.

- *There must be a clear central point for the handling of cyber-intelligence and conducting cyber-defense and cyber-warfare in the intelligence community, with suitable funding and equipment, supported by similar centers of excellence in all other agencies.* They must be clearly linked to both the operational center of cyber-warfare in the Department of Defense and a similar center for conducting cyber-defense and cyber-warfare in the federal law enforcement community. It is easy to assign responsibility, but the issue is to create effective capability.

- *The issue of domestic intelligence gathering and surveillance needs to be revisited.* The very growth of new information systems and data banks poses a threat to traditional rights of privacy and civil liberties without any action by government. At present, however, there does not seem to be a coherent doctrine, body of law, or regulation that examines the interrelationship between intelligence collection, legal surveillance, information exchange within government, and civil rights. Establishing the proper balance is extremely difficult. There is a tendency to minimize government capability without understanding that only government action can help limit abuses in the private sector. "Victims' rights" remain a largely unexplored issue. So does the fact that some forms of attack clearly merit far more federal intervention than others and that the multinational character of many cyber-threats means intelligence gathering cannot stop because U.S. citizens are involved. It may take a decade or more to establish the proper mix of checks and balances, but it is obvious that intelligence gathering and surveillance are the first line of deterrence and defense against all forms of cyber-attack. Thus laws and regulations affecting such activity must be tailored accordingly. A simple loophole that would allow a small intermediary group/agency to approve information sharing between law enforcement and the intelligence community on matters that fall within NIIP (National Information Infrastructure Protection) would be a first step.

- *There must be a clear central organization in the law enforcement community that is trained and equipped to deal with the domestic component of cyber-warfare and respond to large-scale attacks by governments, terrorists, and extremists.* This center must be prepared to conduct such operations in the context of broader economic warfare, conventional warfare, or in parallel with covert or terrorist attacks using large-scale explosive devices, selectively attacking the physical elements in our infrastructure, or using chemical, biological, radiological, or nuclear weapons. It must be given suitable funding and equipment. It is easy to assign responsibility, but the issue is to create effective capability. There must be close ties to a similar cyber-defense and cyber-warfare center of excellence in the intelligence community. It must be clearly linked to a similar center for conducting cyber-defense and cyber-warfare in the Department of Defense.

- *Independent audits of federal vulnerability and competence in critical infrastructure protection.* There is no more reason to assume that federal entities will take proper responsibility for critical infrastructure and cyber-protection that there is to assume they can be trusted to control the efficiency of their accounting and audit procedures. Moreover, the pace of technology change is so rapid that it is not reasonable to assume that most departments and agencies can develop the necessary competence to assess every aspect of their vulnerability. There is a need to either charge the GAO with annual audits of all federal agencies and departments create a federal agency or office charged with the independent auditing of the success of federal efforts to ensure critical infrastructure protecting and computer/information systems. It should also be clear that Secretary or head of a department or agency will have personal responsibility for its performance, and that the chief financial officer will have equal responsibility with the chief information officer. At present, the CIO is often assigned tasks without adequate management support and funding.

- *Create an effective set of programs and future year budget plans to implement an effective federal effort.* This issue has been touched upon earlier, but better management, planning, programming, and budgeting is at least as important to success as any changes in federal leadership and organization far too often, the federal government assigns responsibility and begins program implementation without any clear plan for the end state capabilities it is seeking to develop, and of the cost, manpower, and equipment needed to actually achieve this capability.

    These future year program budgets must be made part of both the central offices in the Department of Defense, intelligence community, and law enforcement community and part of the annual budget submissions of each federal agency. They should involve detailed risk assessments, net assessments of projected capability, and well-defined measures of performance. RDT&E plans should clearly state the estimated total cost to complete development, the estimate deployment time and effectiveness, life cycle cost, and provide a net technical assessment with an analysis of the cost to defeat the project or technology. The functions of the central offices in the Department of Defense, intelligence community, and law enforcement community should include budget review authority over relevant agency program budgets and future year plans. At the same time, clear procedures and contingency funds should be aware to allow rapid and response changes in budgets, plans, and ongoing spending to meet the needs of a constantly evolving technology.

- *Providing adequate funds and reshaping the role of Congress.* The Executive Branch and Congress do not cooperate in funding effective programs, and there is a lack of central review and coordination in both branches. The Congress also seeks to mandate action without providing additional funds and many agency CFOs are unwilling to allocate them. The end result is an impasse that led White House Chief of Staff Tom Podesta to charge on July 17, 2000 that, "We've proposed $90 million to help detect computer attacks, to conduct research on security technology, to hire and train more security experts, and to create an internal expert review team for non-defense agencies. Unfortunately, the Congress still refuses to appropriate one dime to put these initiatives in place. It's time they picked up the pace and provided the protections that are essential to America's cyber-security."[124] It is unclear who is to blame, it is clear that proper efforts are not being funded.

- *Clearly putting the proper burden on state and local governments.* The federal government can help state and local governments protect themselves. It cannot take responsibility for such protection or for any response to compensate for a lack of effective local and state action. At present, there is too much vague talk about partnership, and too little effort to define the strict limits of federal aid and responsibility.

- *Forcing responsibility on the private sector.* The present legal requirements for private and civil sector entities to take full action to defend their information and computer systems, and other parts of the nation's critical infrastructure, remains somewhat ambiguous. Law and regulation should be changed to establish clear requirements that force the immediate disclosure of attacks to law enforcement agencies and the nature of failures in defense. More broadly, private and civil entities should be forced to report such incidents and the level of corporate action to protect critical infrastructure in their annual reports, and in their prospectus. They should also be required to conduct an internal annual audit of their efforts, and an independent external audit similar to an annual financial audit.

- *The U.S. government should work closely with information system providers and manufacturers to assure adequate security features in new products.* Review is needed of how to better ensure that information system providers can be persuaded to give proper weight to protection, prevention, mitigation, and reconstitution capabilities. At present, market forces tend to emphasize speed of change, features, and open access rather than the provision of adequate protection. Also, law enforcement agencies and Internet Service Providers (ISPs) should sit down together and develop a framework covering cooperation during an investigation.

- *A comprehensive review of liability and criminal law relating to critical infrastructure conducted.* While penalties vary by case, current precedents seem to understate the seriousness of cyber-crime and attacks. The same is true of standards for liability. The current standards allow virtually any level of corporate, local, state, or NGO effort to defend infrastructure and information systems to qualify as adequate. Law and regulation should set a high standard requiring state of the art capability and a clearly demonstrated enforcement program to ensure that capabilities are up to date and personnel are properly trained. It should also be unambiguously clear that the chief executive and chief financial officers, and board of directors, will have personal liability and that liability cannot be delegated.

- *What the U.S. cannot defend from attack, it should either insure or require to have private coverage.* There must be clear laws and regulations that specify the level of insurance required against cyber-attack so that no attack can cause panic in financial markets. For example, the destruction of a major corporation's information system could have serious effect on the economy by undermining the faith in financial institutions. As a result, attacks on major players should be viewed as direct attacks on the national infrastructure and subsequently on the national interest.

    Since the government cannot realistically protect every major corporation and NGO, the government should have a policy in place to ensure proper private insurance coverage against information attacks, and that corporations and NGOs take the responsibility to limit their vulnerability, ameiliorate the impact of attacks, and reconstitute their capabilities on a time basis. At the same time, the government should make it clear long before a major attack that it will guarantee remediation and compensation of damage done by a major state or terrorist/extremist attack (similar to an FIDC-like guarantee) in ways that do not reduce corporate or NGO responsibility but make it absolutely clear losses and damage will be compensated for. This could help prevent a panic in financial market or overhyping in the media.

    At the same time, clear standards and regulations should be established for private insurance coverage. One way of ensuring that state and local governments, and private and civil sector entities take the proper self-protection methods is to either encourage or regulate insurance coverage to require proper self-protection measures, regular insurance company audits of performance, raise premiums for inadequate efforts, and deny coverage where the level of action was misreported to the insurance company.

- *Equally important, state and local governments and all elements of the private sector—businesses, utilities, and NGOs—need to explicitly assume responsibility for the vulnerability of their systems and activities, the ability to respond to attacks both during and after the attack, the ability to ameliorate attacks, and the ability to reconstitute their capabilities and/or provide alternative back up systems.* It cannot be emphasized too firmly that any regulations and laws, insurance requirements, and internal efforts that focus only on cyber-defense are so inherently flawed as to be as much a source of future problems as a solution. Pushing the private sector toward more effective defense must be based on pushing it toward the most cost-effective mix of solutions, and not simply toward active cyber-defense.

- *The legal right of self-defense and conditions for offensive action by law enforcement agencies has to be clearly defined.* The law should unmistakably state that all hardware, software, and facilities used for attack are subject to seizure and confiscation, but without losing sight of the fact that arbitrary seizure of such equipment for evidentiary purposes can effectively put a company that was merely used as a relay point out of business. It should also be clear in law that attackers can be counterattacked, as well as negligent or non-responsive providers, under conditions that ensure that the attacker can be properly identified and targeted. There is a risk that organizations could respond with attacks against each other which both see as legitimate self defense, but where the defensive response was actually instigated by an unattributable third party.

- *Solving the person power issue and ensuring that the federal government can obtain and retain the proper expertise.* Generational problems exist at all levels in recruiting, training, and retaining skilled personnel, and in ensuring that managers are selected on the basis of competence and not seniority. Current salaries generally lag far behind the private sector and often tend to be adequate only to retain the incompetent and noncompetitive. There may well be a need for exempted service positions in many critical areas. Another problem that the government shares with the private sector is that most information security professionals are stove piped and rarely find themselves in the management chain. As a result there is nowhere for them to go within the organization and so there is no incentive other than money to stay in a given job.

This may seem to be a daunting list of requirements, and related issues and complications. The fact is, however, that the U.S.—like other nations—has little choice. It must learn to cope with the impact of fundamental changes in technology, information systems, communications, government operations, and the global economy. Given the pace of change, both the threat and the U.S. reaction will be in an almost constant state of evolution, and "business as usual" is simply an impossible alternative.

The key to success may ultimately be for the U.S. government to focus on only those threats that truly threaten the nation. Cyber-war is a case in point, as is high-level cyber-terrorism. So are efforts to create effective international cooperation in limiting all forms of cyber-attack,

The present focus many federal agencies have on cracking/hacking, cyber-crime, and low-level cyber-terrorism is a logical and unavoidable product of federal responsibilities in law enforcement, in ensuring the smooth function of government, and in regulating many areas of civil activity. All of these functions must continue. At the same time, there seems to be no practical way in which the federal government can protect most state and local government use of information systems, private sector activity, or NGOs. Any such effort is almost certain to have illusory success at best. Ultimately, state and local governments, commercial entities, and NGOs must take full responsibility for the vulnerability of their systems and operations, their defense and protection, damage limitation, and reconstitution, and this must involve civil and criminal liability.

Notes

1. Last year, a total of 22,144 "attacks" were detected on Defense Department networks, up from 5,844 in 1998. ("Hacking of Pentagon Computers Persists," *Washington Post*, August 9, 2000).

2. A recent study carried out by the German government showed that the number of Internet home pages for German right-wing extremists grew significantly from 200 in 1998 to 330 in 1999. The German government also has a continuing effort to try to use international law to close down German-language Web sites with Nazi and far-right literature abroad.

3. President's Commission on Critical Infrastructure Protection, pp. 15–16.

4. President's Commission on Critical Infrastructure Protection, p. 17.

5. "Root" access refers to having system administrator privileges on UNIX based servers and workstations. It is used here generically to describe similar access levels on systems running Windows and other operating systems.

6. Statement for the Record of Michael A. Vatis Director, National Infrastructure Protection Center, October 1999 Before the Senate Judiciary Committee Subcommittee on Terrorism. October 6, 1999. Federal Bureau of Investigation on NIPC Cyber Threat Assessment, http://www.fbi.gov/pressrm/congress/congress99/nipc10-6.htm accessed 06/14/00.

7. Statement for the Record of Michael A. Vatis Director, National Infrastructure Protection Center, October 1999 Before the Senate Judiciary Committee Subcommittee on Terrorism. October 6, 1999.

8. The book referred to is the "Unrestricted Warfare" by Qiao Liang and Wang Xiangsui published by PLA Literature and Arts Publishing House, February 1999, Beijing, China. Methods of warfare proposed in this book include

hacking into Web sites, targeting financial institutions, engaging in terrorism, and using the media, to name only a few. The authors were two senior colonels from the younger generation of Chinese military officers. In an interview with Zhongguo Qingnian Bao, Qiao stated that "the first rule of unrestricted warfare is that there are no rules, with nothing forbidden" (FBIS translation of the interview, OW2807114599).

9. Statement for the Record of Michael A. Vatis Director, National Infrastructure Protection Center, October 1999 Before the Senate Judiciary Committee Subcommittee on Terrorism. October 6, 1999. Federal Bureau of Investigation on NIPC Cyber Threat Assessment, October 1999 Before the Senate Judiciary Committee Subcommittee on Terrorism http://www.fbi.gov/pressrm/congress/congress99/nipc10-6.htm accessed 06/14/00.

10. Statement for the Record of Michael A. Vatis Director, National Infrastructure Protection Center, October 1999 Before the Senate Judiciary Committee Subcommittee on Terrorism. October 6, 1999. Federal Bureau of Investigation on NIPC Cyber Threat Assessment, October 1999 Before the Senate Judiciary Committee Subcommittee on Terrorism http://www.fbi.gov/pressrm/congress/congress99/nipc10-6.htm accessed 06/14/00.

11. National Intelligence Council, *Global Trends 2015: A Dialogue About the Future With Nongovernment Experts*, NIC 2000–02, December 2000 http://www.odci.gov/cia/publications/globaltrends2015/index.html.

12. Chapter 8.

13. Prepared joint statement on the Kosovo After Action Review presented by Secretary of Defense William S. Cohen and Gen. Henry H. Shelton, Chairman of the Joint Chiefs of Staff, before the Senate Armed Services Committee, October 14, 1999.

14. This section is based largely on interviews and *Aviation Week and Space Technology*, September 1, 1999, p. 31.

15. Rebecca Grant, "The Kosovo Campaign: Aerospace Power Made it Work," Arlington, Air Force Association, September 1999, p. 15.

16. *Aviation Week and Space Technology*, November 8, 1999, pp. 81–82.

17. *Aviation Week and Space Technology*, November 1, 1999, pp. 33–36.

18. *Aviation Week and Space Technology*, November 1, 1999, pp. 33–36.

19. *Aviation Week and Space Technology*, November 8, 1999, pp. 81–82.

20. *Aviation Week and Space Technology*, November 8, 1999, pp. 81–82.

21. *Washington Post*, November 8, 1999, pp. A-1 and A-10.

22. Ibid.

23. Statement for the Record before the Joint Economic Committee on Cyber Threats and the U.S. Economy by John A. Serabian Jr., Information Operations Issue Manager, CIA. 02/23/2000.

24. Statement for the Record before the Joint Economic Committee on Cyber Threats and the U.S. Economy by John A. Serabian Jr., Information Operations Issue Manager, CIA. 02/23/2000.

25. Statement for the Record before the Joint Economic Committee on Cyber Threats and the U.S. Economy by John A. Serabian Jr., Information Operations Issue Manager, CIA. 02/23/2000.

26. *Congressional Record.* 2000. 106th Cong., 2nd sess., Vol. 146, Nos. 27–28.

27. For more detailed information on the Rome Labs incident consult the testimony given in front of the U.S. Senate Permanent Subcommittee on Investigations Committee on Government Affairs, May 22, 1996 at the hearing on "Security in Cyberspace."

28. At the request of Senator Nunn, the Government Accounting Office conducted an additional damage assessment and released the report number AIMD-96-84 titled "Information Security, Computer Attacks at Department of Defense Pose Increasing Risks," 05/22/96.

29. CSI Press Release "Issues and Trends: 2000 CSI/FBI Computer Crime and Security Survey" March 22, 2000. http://www.gocsi.com/prelea_000321.htm accessed 07/07/00.

30. CSI Press Release "Issues and Trends: 2000 CSI/FBI Computer Crime and Security Survey" March 22, 2000. http://www.gocsi.com/prelea_000321.htm accessed 07/07/00.

31. CSI Press Release "Issues and Trends: 2000 CSI/FBI Computer Crime and Security Survey" March 22, 2000. http://www.gocsi.com/prelea_000321.htm accessed 07/07/00.

32. "Internet Security Issues: Testimony of Richard D. Perthia, Director, CERT Centers, before the US Senate Judiciary Committee," http://www.cert.org/congressional_testimony/Perthia_testimony25May00.html accessed 7/11/00.

33. "Internet Security Issues: Testimony of Richard D. Perthia, Director, CERT Centers, before the US Senate Judiciary Committee," http://www.cert.org/congressional_testimony/Perthia_testimony25May00.html accessed 7/11/00.

34. "Internet Security Issues: Testimony of Richard D. Perthia, Director, CERT Centers, before the US Senate Judiciary Committee," http://www.cert.org/congressional_testimony/Perthia_testimony25May00.html accessed 7/11/00.

35. "Internet Security Issues: Testimony of Richard D. Perthia, Director, CERT Centers, before the US Senate Judiciary Committee," http://www.cert.org/congressional_testimony/Perthia_testimony25May00.html accessed 7/11/00.

36. "Internet Security Issues: Testimony of Richard D. Perthia, Director, CERT Centers, before the US Senate Judiciary Committee," http://www.cert.org/congressional_testimony/Perthia_testimony25May00.html accessed 7/11/00.

37. "Cybercrime . . . Cyberterrorism . . . Cyberwarfare. . . ." CSIS Task Force Report. 1998.

38. "Computer Security Act of 1987" http://thomas.loc.gov/cgi-bin/bdque.

39. "Paperwork Reduction Act or 1995" http://frwebgate.access.gpo.gov/cgi...4_cong_public_laws&docid=publ13.104 accessed 07/05/00.

40. "Information Technology Management Reform Act" 1996 http://www.rdc.noaa.gov/~irm/div-e.htm accessed 07/05/00.

41. Executive Order 13010, July 15, 1996 http://www.ciao.gov/PCCIP/eo13010.pdf accessed June 20, 2000.

42. PCCIP Executive Summary, October 1997.

43. PCCIP Executive Summary http://www.ciao.gov/PCCIP/summary.html accessed June 23.

44. PCCIP Executive Summary.

45. WHITE PAPER: The Clinton Administration's Policy on Critical Infrastructure Protection: Presidential Decision Directive-63, May 22, 1998.

46. Presidential Decision Directive 63.

47. White House Fact Sheet "Promoting Cyber Security for the 21st Century." 01/07/00.

48. White House Fact Sheet "Promoting Cyber Security for the 21st Century." 01/07/00.

49. "National Plan for Information Systems Protection" pp. 6–7.

50. Critical Infrastructure Protection: Comments on the National Plan for Information Systems Protection (Statement/Record, 02/01/00, GAO/T-AIMD-00-72) pp. 1–2.

51. Critical Infrastructure Protection: Comments on the National Plan for Information Systems Protection (Statement/Record, 02/01/00, GAO/T-AIMD-00-72) p. 4.

52. Critical Infrastructure Protection: Comments on the National Plan for Information Systems Protection (Statement/Record, 02/01/00, GAO/T-AIMD-00-72) p. 5.

53. United States General Accounting Office (GAO), "Comments on the National Plan for Information Systems Protection, "Statement for the Record by Jack L. Brock, Jr., Director, Governmentwide and Defense Information Systems Accounting and Information Management Division, Testimony Before the Subcommittee on Technology, Terrorism and Government Information, Committee on the Judiciary, U.S. Senate, February 1, 2000.

54. "U.S. Army Kick-starts Cyberwar Machine," http://www.nwfusion.com/news/2000/1120cyberattack.html?nf accessed 12/1/00.

55. "National Plan. . . ." p. 122.

56. "Annual Report to Congress on Combating Terrorism: Including Defense against Weapons of Mass Destruction/Domestic Preparedness and Critical Infrastructure Protection" May 18, 2000, p. 6.

57. "National Plan for Information Systems Protection, Version One" January 2000, p. 126.

58. "Annual Report to Congress on Combating Terrorism: Including Defense against Weapons of Mass Destruction/Domestic Preparedness and Critical Infrastructure Protection" May 18, 2000, p. 3.

59. "Annual Report to Congress on Combating Terrorism: Including Defense against Weapons of Mass Destruction/Domestic Preparedness and Critical Infrastructure Protection" May 18, 2000, p. 7.

60. "Annual Report to Congress on Combating Terrorism: Including Defense against Weapons of Mass Destruction/Domestic Preparedness and Critical Infrastructure Protection" May 18, 2000, pp. 17–18.

61. "Annual Report to Congress on Combating Terrorism: Including Defense against Weapons of Mass Destruction/Domestic Preparedness and Critical Infrastructure Protection" May 18, 2000, p. 78.

62. "Annual Report to Congress on Combating Terrorism: Including

Defense against Weapons of Mass Destruction/Domestic Preparedness and Critical Infrastructure Protection" May 18, 2000, p. 17.

63. "Annual Report to Congress on Combating Terrorism: Including Defense against Weapons of Mass Destruction/Domestic Preparedness and Critical Infrastructure Protection" May 18, 2000, p. 70.

64. "Annual Report to Congress on Combating Terrorism: Including Defense against Weapons of Mass Destruction/Domestic Preparedness and Critical Infrastructure Protection" May 18, 2000, p. 69.

65. "Annual Report to Congress on Combating Terrorism: Including Defense against Weapons of Mass Destruction/Domestic Preparedness and Critical Infrastructure Protection" May 18, 2000, p. 23.

66. "Annual Report to Congress on Combating Terrorism: Including Defense against Weapons of Mass Destruction/Domestic Preparedness and Critical Infrastructure Protection" May 18, 2000, pp. 23–24.

67. "Annual Report to Congress on Combating Terrorism: Including Defense against Weapons of Mass Destruction/Domestic Preparedness and Critical Infrastructure Protection" May 18, 2000, p. 23.

68. "Annual Report to Congress on Combating Terrorism: Including Defense against Weapons of Mass Destruction/Domestic Preparedness and Critical Infrastructure Protection" May 18, 2000, p. 18.

69. "Annual Report to Congress on Combating Terrorism: Including Defense against Weapons of Mass Destruction/Domestic Preparedness and Critical Infrastructure Protection" May 18, 2000, pp. 23–24.

70. "Annual Report to Congress on Combating Terrorism: Including Defense against Weapons of Mass Destruction/Domestic Preparedness and Critical Infrastructure Protection" May 18, 2000, p. 24.

71. "Annual Report to Congress on Combating Terrorism: Including Defense against Weapons of Mass Destruction/Domestic Preparedness and Critical Infrastructure Protection" May 18, 2000, p. 24.

72. "Annual Report to Congress on Combating Terrorism: Including Defense against Weapons of Mass Destruction/Domestic Preparedness and Critical Infrastructure Protection" May 18, 2000, pp. 26–27.

73. "Annual Report to Congress on Combating Terrorism: Including Defense against Weapons of Mass Destruction/Domestic Preparedness and Critical Infrastructure Protection" May 18, 2000, p. 27.

74. "Annual Report to Congress on Combating Terrorism: Including Defense against Weapons of Mass Destruction/Domestic Preparedness and Critical Infrastructure Protection" May 18, 2000, p. 37.

75. Federal Information Security: Actions Needed to Address Widespread Weaknesses (GAO/T-AIMD-00-135, March 29, 2000) p. 2.

76. "Annual Report to Congress on Combating Terrorism: Including Defense against Weapons of Mass Destruction/Domestic Preparedness and Critical Infrastructure Protection" May 18, 2000, p. 69.

77. "Annual Report to Congress on Combating Terrorism: Including Defense against Weapons of Mass Destruction/Domestic Preparedness and Critical Infrastructure Protection" May 18, 2000, p. 71.

78. "Annual Report to Congress on Combating Terrorism: Including Defense against Weapons of Mass Destruction/Domestic Preparedness and Critical Infrastructure Protection" May 18, 2000, p. 69.

79. "Annual Report to Congress on Combating Terrorism: Including Defense against Weapons of Mass Destruction/Domestic Preparedness and Critical Infrastructure Protection" May 18, 2000, p. 71.

80. "Annual Report to Congress on Combating Terrorism: Including Defense against Weapons of Mass Destruction/Domestic Preparedness and Critical Infrastructure Protection" May 18, 2000, p. 30.

81. "Annual Report to Congress on Combating Terrorism: Including Defense against Weapons of Mass Destruction/Domestic Preparedness and Critical Infrastructure Protection" May 18, 2000, pp. 71–72.

82. *Information Security: Many NASA Mission-Critical Systems Face Serious Risks* (GAO/AIMD-99-47, May 20, 1999) p. 1.

83. *Information Security: Many NASA Mission-Critical Systems Face Serious Risks* (GAO/AIMD-99-47, May 20, 1999) p. 2.

84. *Information Security: Many NASA Mission-Critical Systems Face Serious Risks* (GAO/AIMD-99-47, May 20, 1999) p. 2.

85. *Information Security: Many NASA Mission-Critical Systems Face Serious Risks* (GAO/AIMD-99-47, May 20, 1999) pp. 16–17.

86. "Annual Report to Congress on Combating Terrorism: Including Defense against Weapons of Mass Destruction/Domestic Preparedness and Critical Infrastructure Protection" May 18, 2000, pp. 72, 75.

87. "Annual Report to Congress on Combating Terrorism: Including Defense against Weapons of Mass Destruction/Domestic Preparedness and Critical Infrastructure Protection" May 18, 2000, p. 40.

88. "Annual Report to Congress on Combating Terrorism: Including Defense against Weapons of Mass Destruction/Domestic Preparedness and Critical Infrastructure Protection" May 18, 2000, p. 41.

89. Walter Pincus, "Defense Department Computers Vulnerable to Attack," *Washington Post*, December 8, 2000, Internet edition.

90. Walter Pincus, "Defense Department Computers Vulnerable to Attack," *Washington Post*, December 8, 2000, Internet edition.

91. http://www.defenselink.mil/pubs/ *Depsecweb.pdf*.

92. Walter Pincus, "Defense Department Computers Vulnerable to Attack," *Washington Post*, December 8, 2000, Internet edition.

93. Walter Pincus, "Defense Department Computers Vulnerable to Attack," *Washington Post*, December 8, 2000, Internet edition.

94. Walter Pincus, "Defense Department Computers Vulnerable to Attack," *Washington Post*, December 8, 2000, Internet edition.

95. Gerry J. Gilmore, "DoD Taps Reservists To Fill New Info Ops Units," American Forces Press Service, December 8, 2000.

96. GAO/AIMD-99-107 "DoD Information Security: Serious Weaknesses Continue to Place Defense Operations at Risk," August 1999, pp. 14–15.

97. GAO/AIMD-99-107 "DoD Information Security: Serious Weaknesses

Continue to Place Defense Operations at Risk," August 1999, Appendix I. pp. 24–25.

98. GAO/AIMD-99-107 "DoD Information Security: Serious Weaknesses Continue to Place Defense Operations at Risk," August 1999, pp. 17–18.

99. GAO/AIMD-99-107 "DoD Information Security: Serious Weaknesses Continue to Place Defense Operations at Risk," August 1999, p. 8.

100. GAO/AIMD-99-107 "DoD Information Security: Serious Weaknesses Continue to Place Defense Operations at Risk," August 1999, p. 3.

101. GAO/AIMD-99-107 "DoD Information Security: Serious Weaknesses Continue to Place Defense Operations at Risk," August 1999, p. 5.

102. GAO/AIMD-99-107 "DoD Information Security: Serious Weaknesses Continue to Place Defense Operations at Risk," August 1999, pp. 8–12.

103. GAO/AIMD-99-107 "DoD Information Security: Serious Weaknesses Continue to Place Defense Operations at Risk," August 1999, p. 12.

104. GAO/AIMD-99-107 "DoD Information Security: Serious Weaknesses Continue to Place Defense Operations at Risk," August 1999, p. 13.

105. GAO/AIMD-99-107 "DoD Information Security: Serious Weaknesses Continue to Place Defense Operations at Risk," August 1999, p. 13.

106. GAO/AIMD-99-107 "DoD Information Security: Serious Weaknesses Continue to Place Defense Operations at Risk," August 1999, p. 14.

107. Federal Information Security: Actions Needed to Address Widespread Weaknesses (GAO/T-AIMD-00-135, March 29, 2000) p. 3.

108. "Annual Report to Congress on Combating Terrorism: Including Defense against Weapons of Mass Destruction/Domestic Preparedness and Critical Infrastructure Protection" May 18, 2000, pp. 34–35.

109. "Annual Report to Congress on Combating Terrorism: Including Defense against Weapons of Mass Destruction/Domestic Preparedness and Critical Infrastructure Protection" May 18, 2000, p. 73.

110. Federal Information Security: Actions Needed to Address Widespread Weaknesses (GAO/T-AIMD-00-135, March 29, 2000) p. 3.

111. "Testimony, Before the House Subcommittee on Government Management, Information and Technology, Committee on Government Reform on Actions Needed to Address Widespread Weaknesses," delivered by Jack L. Brock Jr., Director, Governmentwide and Defense Information Systems Accounting and Information Management Division, March 29, 2000, pp. 3–5.

112. "Testimony, Before the House Subcommittee on Government Management, Information and Technology, Committee on Government Reform on Actions Needed to Address Widespread Weaknesses," delivered by Jack L. Brock Jr., Director, Governmentwide and Defense Information Systems Accounting and Information Management Division, March 29, 2000, p. 5.

113. "Testimony, Before the House Subcommittee on Government Management, Information and Technology, Committee on Government Reform on Actions Needed to Address Widespread Weaknesses," delivered by Jack L. Brock Jr., Director, Governmentwide and Defense Information Systems Accounting and Information Management Division, March 29, 2000, p. 6.

114. "Testimony, Before the House Subcommittee on Government Management, Information and Technology, Committee on Government Reform on Actions Needed to Address Widespread Weaknesses," delivered by Jack L. Brock Jr., Director, Governmentwide and Defense Information Systems Accounting and Information Management Division, March 29, 2000, p. 6.

115. "Testimony, Before the House Subcommittee on Government Management, Information and Technology, Committee on Government Reform on Actions Needed to Address Widespread Weaknesses," delivered by Jack L. Brock Jr., Director, Governmentwide and Defense Information Systems Accounting and Information Management Division, March 29, 2000, p. 7.

116. "Testimony, Before the House Subcommittee on Government Management, Information and Technology, Committee on Government Reform on Actions Needed to Address Widespread Weaknesses," delivered by Jack L. Brock Jr., Director, Governmentwide and Defense Information Systems Accounting and information Management Division, March 29, 2000, p. 7.

117. "Testimony, Before the House Subcommittee on Government Management, Information and Technology, Committee on Government Reform on Actions Needed to Address Widespread Weaknesses," delivered by Jack L. Brock Jr., Director, Governmentwide and Defense Information Systems Accounting and Information Management Division, March 29, 2000, p. 7.

118. "Testimony, Before the House Subcommittee on Government Management, Information and Technology, Committee on Government Reform on Actions Needed to Address Widespread Weaknesses," delivered by Jack L. Brock Jr., Director, Governmentwide and Defense Information Systems Accounting and Information Management Division, March 29, 2000, p. 8.

119. "Testimony, Before the House Subcommittee on Government Management, Information and Technology, Committee on Government Reform on Actions Needed to Address Widespread Weaknesses," delivered by Jack L. Brock Jr., Director, Governmentwide and Defense Information Systems Accounting and Information Management Division, March 29, 2000, p. 8.

120. Information Security: Comments on Proposed Government Information Act of 1999 (Testimony, 03/02/2000, GAO/T-AIMD-00-107).

121. T-AIM-00-107.

122. Reuters, December 6, 2000, 1529.

123. The Convention has grown out of Recommendation N° R (85) 10 concerning the practical application of the European Convention on Mutual Assistance in Criminal Matters in respect of letters rogatory for the interception of telecommunications, Recommendation N° R (88) 2 on piracy in the field of copyright and neighboring rights as well as Recommendation N° R (89) 9 on computer-related crime providing guidelines for national legislatures concerning the definition of certain computer crimes and Recommendation N° R (95) 13 concerning problems of criminal procedural law connected with Information Technology; It relates to Resolution No. 1 adopted by the European Ministers of Justice at their 21st Conference (Prague, June 1997), which recommended the Committee of Ministers to support the work carried out by the European Committee on Crime Problems (CDPC) on cyber-crime in order to bring

domestic criminal law provisions closer to each other and enable the use of effective means of investigation concerning such offences, as well as to Resolution N° 3 adopted at the 23rd Conference of the European Ministers of Justice (London, June 2000), which encouraged the negotiating parties to pursue their efforts with a view to finding appropriate solutions so as to enable the largest possible number of States to become parties to the Convention and acknowledged the need for a swift and efficient system of international co-operation, which duly takes into account the specific requirements of the fight against cyber-crime; It also relates to the Action Plan adopted by the Heads of State and Government of the Council of Europe, on the occasion of their Second Summit (Strasbourg, 10–11 October 1997), to seek common responses to the development of the new information technologies, based on the standards and values of the Council of Europe. See conventions.coe.int/treaty/EN/cadreprojets.htm.

124. The White House, Office of the Press Secretary, For Immediate Release, July 18, 2000. As prepared for delivery, "REMARKS BY THE PRESIDENT'S CHIEF OF STAFF JOHN D. PODESTA ON ELECTRONIC PRIVACY TO NATIONAL PRESS CLUB," Washington, July 17, 2000.

About the Authors

ANTHONY H. CORDESMAN is Co-Director of the Middle East Program at the Center for Strategic and International Studies, and a special consultant on military affairs for ABC News. The author of numerous books on international security issues, he has served in senior positions for the secretary of defense, NATO, and the U.S. Senate.

JUSTIN G. CORDESMAN is Vice President for Operations at InterTech Technologies Inc., where he has an extensive background managing information securities programs for government and commercial clients.